D1231050

# The Challenge
# to Our Cultural Heritage

DISCARDED

Proceedings of a Conference

on Cultural Preservation

Washington, D.C., 8–10 April 1984

# The Challenge

# to Our Cultural Heritage

## *Why Preserve the Past?*

Edited by Yudhishthir Raj Isar

Co-sponsored by United Nations Educational,
Scientific and Cultural Organization (Unesco)
and Smithsonian Institution in cooperation with
The United States Committee of the International
Council on Monuments and Sites (US/ICOMOS)
and The National Trust for Historic Preservation

SMITHSONIAN INSTITUTION PRESS

Washington, D.C.   London

UNESCO   Paris

JEROME LIBRARY BOWLING GREEN STATE UNIVERSITY

First published 1986
by the United Nations Educational,
Scientific and Cultural Organization
7 Place de Fontenoy, 75700 Paris, France
and
Smithsonian Institution
Washington, D.C.

Copyright © Unesco 1986

The general editor prepared the proceedings of this
international conference for publication. The orthographic
preferences of individual contributors have been retained with
regard to American and British spelling and the transliteration
of foreign place names. Documentation and illustrations,
except where otherwise noted in captions, were provided
by the contributors.

The ideas and opinions expressed in this book are those of the
authors and do not necessarily represent the views of Unesco.

**Library of Congress Cataloging-in-Publication Data**
    The challenge to our cultural heritage.
    1. Historic sites—Conservation and restoration—
Congresses. 2. Cultural property, Protection of—
Congresses. 3. Architecture—Conservation and
restoration—Congresses. I. Isar, Yudhishthir Raj.
II. Title.
CC135.C55 1984        363.6'9        86-600111
ISBN 0-87474-543-8 (Smithsonian)
ISBN 92-3-102370-5 (Unesco)

*Cover Illustrations*
*Top:* Pagoda roofs, Kathmandu, Nepal. Photo: Unesco/Cart.
*Middle:* Small Temple of Abu Simbel, Egypt. Photo: Unesco/
Nenadovic.
*Bottom:* Amr Ibn El Aass mosque, Cairo. Photo: G. Lekegian,
courtesy Fogg Art Museum, Harvard University

∞ The paper used in this publication
   meets the minimum requirements
   of the American National Standard
   for Permanence of Paper for Printed
   Library Materials Z39.48-1984.

# Contents

5

# Foreword

PAUL N. PERROT

Enthusiasm for historic preservation is manifest now in virtually every part of the world. Yet despite enormous strides in conservation technology, increasing awareness on the part of public and private authorities, and an ever-growing commitment of funds to the cause of historic preservation, our collective heritage is perhaps under greater jeopardy today than at any time in the past. This is particularly true in economically less developed nations that are aspiring to parity with their more fortunate, distant neighbors.

The gravity of heritage protection issues—and the complex economic, political, geographic, climatic, and psychological questions they raise—suggested the time had come to stimulate greater awareness among the general public, particularly on the North American continent. The conference summarized in this volume was suggested by Unesco as a means of introducing the North American press to some of the most advanced theories currently being practiced in various parts of the world. Its aim was to inform as well as alert journalists to the urgent need for greater public awareness and more aggressive governmental action.

Unesco has a long history of concern for the built environment and for the irreplaceable heritage it represents. From its inception, Unesco has worked both independently and in cooperation with other organizations to mobilize the international community. It has consistently supported programs of mutual aid in order to preserve for future generations irreplaceable parts of a cultural past that, though it may be the glory of a single country or people, is the heritage of all.

In cooperation with the Smithsonian Institution, an organization founded "for the increase and diffusion of knowledge among men," Unesco joined with the International Council on Monuments and Sites (ICOMOS) and its American committee, US/ICOMOS, and the U.S. National Trust for Historic Preservation to sponsor the gathering summarized in these pages.

The organizers had a single goal: to bring together in a common arena the most active and best-informed experts on historic preservation and practitioners concerned with and sympathetic to a complex range of economic, sociological, and technological questions.

From the beginning the effort was marked by a desire to collaborate, and this collaboration remained close and effective from the earliest planning stage to the concluding sessions.

The partners in this endeavor cooperated as if they were one, and they received the warmest support from all participants.

That this conference came at such a difficult period in Unesco's history is unfortunate since this may have overshadowed, in the eyes of some, the raison d'être for the meeting. Yet the conference demonstrated fully the wisdom and value of Unesco's policies and practices in the field of historic preservation and the protection of our collective heritage.

It is the hope of the organizers that this conference will stimulate a further assessment of needs and the commitment of additional resources, psychic and physical, for heritage protection. We must preserve values whose importance is inestimable, representing achievements going back to the dawn of civilization as we know it. Can there be greater testimony to our belief in the future than our respect for and preservation of a collective past?

# Preface

In April 1984 Unesco, the Smithsonian Institution, the U.S. Committee of the International Council on Monuments and Sites (US/ICOMOS), and the U.S. National Trust for Historic Preservation organized a conference for journalists entitled "The Challenge to Our Cultural Heritage: Why Preserve the Past?"

The sponsors brought together in Washington, D.C., some thirty distinguished professionals—architect-restorers, architectural historians, urban planners, cultural heritage administrators, and museum curators from fourteen different countries—and an almost equal number of North American journalists. The Smithsonian Institution hosted the conference and its Secretary, S. Dillon Ripley, delivered the keynote address. Amadou-Mahtar M'Bow, Director-General of Unesco, gave the closing address at a banquet he hosted at the Air and Space Museum, where the participants were joined by a number of distinguished representatives of Washington's cultural institutions and diplomatic corps.

The conference covered a wide range of topics. It was intended to contribute to two of Unesco's basic objectives: first, the wider international dissemination and sharing of specialized knowledge and, second, the strengthening of public awareness of the dangers to the cultural heritage of humanity and of the international community's efforts to combat them. Although this aspect of Unesco's work is among the most clearly understood and appreciated by the public at large, it had been recognized for some time that neither the full dimension of the challenges facing the cultural heritage nor the scope of international response (including the active and significant participation of institutions and specialists in the United States and Canada) were adequately known in North America.

The international record of the Smithsonian Institution is rich in the heritage preservation area. So too is its history of cooperation with Unesco. Both organizations felt that a meeting of minds and concerned specializations, mounted specifically for an audience of professional communicators, would help close the information gap.

Individual North American professionals, active in heritage preservation at the international level, also welcomed this opportunity to
give wider visibility to their long commitment. The principal conduits
for this international participation were the American and Canadian
members of ICOMOS, whose next triannual general conference will
take place in Washington, D.C., in 1987. The U.S. Committee of
ICOMOS was joined by the National Trust for Historic Preservation.
Both organizations are conscious of the great strides historic preservation has made in the last decade, yet are ever eager to promote not
only international recognition of the unique qualities of the preservation movement on the North American continent, but also even
greater public commitment to a rich variety of programmes to preserve
archaeological, architectural, and historical sites.

Thanks to the rapport created with the participating journalists,
the conference succeeded in achieving its immediate public information goals. It yielded fresh insights into the complexities of heritage
protection in developing countries, where resources are pitifully scarce
in the face of unprecedented technological pressures. The participants
were introduced to some of the spectacular successes of international
cooperation, in which professional expertise and financial support
from both public and private American institutions have long played
a crucial role. They were also provided with detailed information on
preservation practice in the United States and Canada, which highlighted the values, principles, and methods that distinguish it from
efforts undertaken elsewhere.

In addition to its immediate information-bearing function, the
conference also contributed to the international exchange of knowledge and experience. Because they were speaking to a nonspecialized
but highly alert audience, the panelists made sure their presentations
combined scholarly depth with clarity, and comprehensiveness with
concision. New contacts were made and old associations renewed.
Differences of interpretation and method were compared and assessed
and fresh insights gained. Some basic conceptual questions were
raised: What place can be assigned to the preservation of the material
vestiges of a society's past in relation to a notion of "modernity"
appropriate to the needs, aspirations, and sensibilities of our time?
What are the economic and social costs of a preservationist stance
and how can they be met? How can preservation's case be argued
against the conflicting priorities of finance ministries and budget
directors? How can the preservation of the built environment, particularly historic city centres, be reconciled with urban development
needs? How can we use modern technology together with traditional

know-how to make optimum use of severely limited resources? How does present-day illicit traffic in cultural property impoverish a shared heritage, and what can be done to stop it? How can we best ensure a wide measure of private support and participation in the safeguarding of an inheritance common to all?

This volume of conference papers represents another contribution to the search for solutions to these problems. The collection brings together a selection of the written papers presented. Several participants contributed extempore; their lively oral presentations did not lend themselves easily to written form. The communications were reorganized by the editor into five sections: Is There a Collision Course between Preservation and Modernization?; Mobilizing Resources for Preservation; Harnessing Science and Technology: Realities and Paradoxes; Evolving Concepts and Practices; and The Scourge of Illicit Traffic in Cultural Property.

Underlying the discussion of these topics was the recognition of a paradoxical reality: the popularity of heritage preservation is also the cause of one of its most difficult dilemmas. The widespread expression of concern for the cultural heritage has led to a massive extension of the heritage concept itself. As more and more phenomena that surround us are recognized as a testimony of the past, acute problems of choice arise. Even the most recent phenomena may be worth preserving: as a bulwark against the increasing impermanence of the modern technological environment or as a symbol of cultural identity, or both. But resources are finite; we cannot save everything and also make it accessible to a large public. How should we choose? The question perplexes governments, museum curators, and monument conservators the world over. In industrially developed countries, they are able to organize safeguard activities in a coherent way, armed with public and private infrastructures, trained personnel, and, last but not least, a broad base of commitment among citizens. In the developing world, however, such resources are limited and priorities lie elsewhere.

It must be said here that neither Unesco nor any specialized international organization has ready answers to the problem of choice. Aesthetic criteria evolve constantly; features considered to be historically or ethnographically significant also change over time. Where the international community can help, however, is in the mobilization of national and international resources such as funds, technical support for preservation projects, and public commitment. It can also help individual countries sharpen tools for identifying and understanding (inventories, studies, etc.) the vast cultural heritage awaiting preservation, so that the governments and people themselves can make the necessary choices. Providing cooperation and assistance are therefore fundamental components in Unesco's cultural heritage programme. It is only on the basis of clearer knowledge of the variety and range of the legacy of the past that each country can come closer to a selective policy for saving some elements for posterity while sacrificing others.

# Keynote Address

S. DILLON RIPLEY

It is a great pleasure indeed to have the opportunity of welcoming those who have come to this Unesco/Smithsonian-sponsored conference on historic preservation. The ever-present danger to our cultural heritage is something that Unesco was essentially founded to oversee and, if possible, to help control. The Smithsonian Institution, founded in 1846 "for the increase and diffusion of knowledge among men," is essentially a foundation devoted to research and the dissemination of information within, but not of the government. It was founded as a result of a bequest of an English scientist, with money left by him in his will, to create in Washington, the capital city, an institution that could act as a cultural and research center based primarily on private support.

Of course over the years, with the creation of buildings that were open to the public as mandated by the Congress in accepting this unique bequest, the expense of maintaining collections for the public and supporting buildings that required security and protection, as well as library facilities, maintenance, and accessibility to large numbers of people, meant that the Institution quickly developed a series of museumlike functions far exceeding the capacity of the income for research and publication. After some ten years of existence, the Smithsonian Institution began to receive a small annual subvention for these purposes from the government. In addition an annual report, which the government had required in accepting the bequest, was prepared, and this too was supported by a subvention for publication. Over the years the Institution has grown steadily as an amalgam of privately and publicly supported activities, making it unique among our institutions of higher education and learning.

Of course nowadays our government has developed foundations for granting funds for education and for a variety of cultural activities much akin to the original concept of the Smithsonian. However, with the Smithsonian's additional administrative organization, namely a Board of Regents responsible for the control of these funds, the Congress and the executive branch of our government have reinforced the concept of an independent foundation carrying out the mission of increase and diffusion. Thus sheltered from the ebb and flow of partisan feelings or political overtones, the Institution has managed for more than a hundred years to maintain a sense of academic integrity and devotion to the causes for which it was created.

The Smithsonian's concern with activities related to the pursuits of Unesco began already with the development of studies in archaeology and anthropology in the late 1840s. One of our first publications, issued in 1849, was on the excavation of Native American Indian mounds and burial sites in the western and southwestern states of the Union. Another early publication was on linguistics, a grammar of the Yoruba language of that tribe of western Africa. Almost at once, the Smithsonian's activities for increasing the diffusion of knowledge became international through an elaborate correspondence maintained by its Secretary with national institutes, national libraries, academies of learning, and kindred societies around the world. Thus in 1965, when the Institution's celebration of the two-hundredth anniversary of the birth of James Smithson coincided with the first meeting of the International Council of Museums held in Washington, some 700 delegates representing academies and societies from around the world came to the United States for a splendid ceremony reinforcing the unique academic character of this Institution.

With the founding of Unesco after World War II and the emphasis on international understanding of cultural concerns and priorities, the Smithsonian gradually entered into correspondence and exchange with a number of the commissions and activities of the new organization. The creation of the International Council of Museums (ICOM) and two related organizations—the International Council on Monuments and Sites (ICOMOS) and the International Centre for the Study of the Preservation and the Restoration of Cultural Property in Rome (ICCROM)—gave the classic archaeological concerns of the Smithsonian more scope for cooperation. On our side of the water, in the 1950s the Institution embarked on an active program, with sponsorship from the U.S. Department of the Interior's National Park Service, to preserve and record archaeological sites as they were uncovered, especially in our western states, by the construction and road building then taking place. These activities—undertaken before the onset of bulldozers—resulted in a valuable series of archaeological recordings of sites ranging back to early pre-Columbian times.

Accordingly, with the founding of ICOM and the kindred interest of major museums across the United States, the Smithsonian took a natural role in collaboration with ICOM. At our initiative, the

Institution qualified in the 1960s—via Congress's permission—for American fund equivalents held abroad in foreign currencies in some nine or ten countries from the sale of excess grains and food stuffs from the United States. As a result the Institution was able to join actively in campaigns initiated by Unesco and underscored by cooperation from ICOM in the preservation and documentation of archaeological remains in a variety of countries: from the Maghrib east through Egypt and Israel to the northern Mediterranean in Yugoslavia. Additional counterpart funds were made available in India, Pakistan, Burma, and Sri Lanka. When the campaigns were announced by Unesco for the preservation of internationally recognized historic monuments, such as Abu Simbel and its adjunct temples and monuments in Nubia and Moenjodaro—part of the cultural heritage of the world—the Institution was able to represent the United States in soliciting supporting funds from Congress. We have persisted in this effort up to the present day and are still actively engaged in the project to study the ruins of Moenjodaro and to define new methods through conservation techniques. We have especially worked with the International Conservation Center in Rome to counter the migration of salts up through the sun-dried brick and stone of that great monument.

We will persist in this as long as possible with the active cooperation and aid of the government of Pakistan. There are, of course, similar sites and monuments waiting for rescue in India, Nepal, Burma, and Thailand. For these the cultural impetus of Unesco is essential, and we await further cooperative programs. The initiative and will of Unesco's support for restoration and conservation and the cooperation of the countries involved and their sincere dedication to the cause will also depend on time and funds and a comprehension of the importance of international initiatives in the future.

Within the past few years, the Smithsonian has taken on another program that will have important international significance for the future. The subject of conservation reaches far beyond the better-known concerns of art museum departments, such as the restoration of paintings, the preservation of works on paper, bronze disease, and so on. I have already referred to the concern of international organizations with the conservation of whole buildings or monuments, tombs or edifices, and cities of the past.

As pointed out in a book written by Karl Meyer, which I reviewed some ten years ago, there has been a historic "failure of national and international institutions, including the large museums, to prepare for the future by developing proper conservation programs." As I wrote, "Senator Claiborne Pell of Rhode Island thoughtfully convoked two days of hearings in the United States Senate on the subject of conservation, restoration, and services of museums. For all we know, they were the first ever held on the subject of which most people continue to be entirely unaware."

Like birth control or ecology, Karl Meyer's subject is a fundamental issue in today's world. It is probably susceptible only to international control. And yet to speak of international control "Is to speak plangently like a knell." The past history of antiquities and of ancient civilizations is riddled with examples of destruction, vandalism, and carelessness. Add to that the amazing lack of attention to objects already preserved and collected in museums and one has small chance of being able to guarantee the continuing existence of objects representing our cultural heritage. It is true, of course, as I have written before, that "man created himself even as he created his culture and thereby became dependent on it." If we are not careful, generations in the future will lack any evidence of culture at all as a historical precept. Without the objects garnered in museums, without collections of historic objects maintained in parklike reserves such as the great monuments, the mere persistence of the printed word will not be sufficient to remind younger generations of their heritage.

Seeing is believing, and a vision of great temples, great monuments, and great works of art links the past together and reminds the young that culture persists and is a treasure in itself, for on it depends much of man's future.

As the years have gone by, it has become clearer to all that the works of nature and the works created by man are inseparably intertwined in the general subject of conservation. If we cannot preserve our total environment, we are, of course, at risk ourselves. In the same way, if we cannot preserve the capacity of mankind to maintain cultural traditions and the discipline of the spirit that results from such an appreciation of civilization, then we are as surely lost intellectually as we are physically.

I hope that the work of the Smithsonian in the creation of a vast new museum support center, just completed a little over a year ago near Washington, will provide a training center for conservation, perhaps the largest in the world, in full realization that without conservation as taught in an apprentice system, museums face a diminishing future in terms of the objects of value they can continue to preserve. Paul Perrot, my assistant and kindred spirit in these matters, who served the Smithsonian so well for years and now directs the Virginia Museum of Fine Arts, has been largely responsible since

I retired from ICOM for continuing American representation in that organization. It is his imagination and genius that have promoted our conservation center, helped by Congressional hearings and supporters like Senator Pell. The center is now staffed and equipped, and we hope that in years to come we can produce up to thirty trained conservators a year to fan out through the United States and the world, carrying the torch for this newly conceived concept.

This learning and care started originally in Rome with the conservation center under the direction of Harold Plenderleith. Other colleagues must carry on for all museums and for all cultural restoration projects, indoors or outdoors, around the globe. We are indeed all one in these matters; as Unesco and the United Nations Environmental Program in Nairobi have taught us, we sink or swim together in the effort to preserve not only our environment but the lingering traces and the persistent roots of our cultural evolution. Thinking of the word "culture" reminds me that a few years ago I wrote that the term was "as badly described today as is ecology. Both derive, as words, from subjective approaches of our own selves. Culture stems historically from the increase in brain size of higher primates. Man and his culture evolved simultaneously through a complex series of interlocking, interreacting processes, which we now like to term feedbacks. Primitive forms of art, of religion, and of science also played their part in affecting the development of neural processes and their integration in evolving man. New reaction patterns came with brain enlargement. Man adapts physiologically to his own culture. What is almost certain in all this is that the various components of human culture are now required not only for the survival of man but also for his existential realization."

If man has created his culture, he is, as I said above, dependent on it. Let us remember that "the instant we are born we are prisoners within our environment, within our living apparatus and within our culture." "The voyage [of life] while we are part of it, is much too fascinating" to give up. "Take cultures, for example; cultures vary between communities. They are as various as the degrees of separation between [them]. It is almost certain that this [must] continue to be true [presumably forever]. Then even to look at them, to observe them, is rewarding in itself. How can one be alienated from such diversity?"

It seems to me that one of our maxims in connection with both the work of Unesco in cultural restoration and the work of the Smithsonian itself should be "the importance of the study of two basic confrontations, the impact of man on his environment and the impact of the environment on man—and the effect that objects have upon man, and the influence that man has upon objects. Somewhere within these realms, there are clues to our understanding of ourselves and, I suspect, our survival." These are the principles that the Smithsonian inescapably shares with Unesco. Let us hope that both institutions will manage to preserve these concepts and to focus on them for the essential survival, not only of mankind, but of the institutions themselves.

# Is There a Collision Course between Preservation and Modernization?

# Collision Course
## *Heritage Preservation versus the Demands of Modernization*

YUDHISHTHIR RAJ ISAR

*Inasmuch as it is rooted in tradition, culture has sometimes been regarded as an obstacle to modernization. But far from being a drawback, the fact that countries refuse to lose their identity by accepting alien models should be welcomed both from the national and from the global point of view. For what is rejected never amounts to more than an imitation lacking the authenticity that gives human enterprises their vigour and value. On the other hand—and there are examples to prove it—the conquest of modernity in the Third World Countries can be achieved by other means than the passive adoption of a process copied from foreign models. A people's awareness of its cultural identity can be a force that supports economic development and modernization and gives them a special dynamic quality. Modernity is then regarded as the stage or reactualization of the forms, relationships and symbols constituting the specific style and meaning of a culture, which is reached after a stage of interrogation when obsolete elements are discarded as no longer relevant to comtemporary issues.*[1]

There are several ways of looking at the confrontation between preservation and modernization. In one sense, a question mark is indispensable, signifying our doubts about the validity of assuming there is a collision course. International experience leads us to believe that more and more people are acting and making decisions on the premise that the only effective "modernization" is a process that integrates the heritage of the past.

The word "modernization" also needs qualification. There is a basic difficulty with the notion of "the modern" itself. The *Oxford English Dictionary* defines the word "modern" as follows: "of the present and recent times." Nothing could be more characteristic of the present and recent times than the phenomenal growth of the heritage conservation movement. Heritage conservation is coming to be as-signed a high value in the minds of people everywhere, not just among intellectuals and politicians, but among broad sections of the

21

Philae, Egypt. Detail of
one of the pylons of the
Temple of Isis as it
emerged from the
receding waters of the
Nile in 1959. Unesco
experts helped plan the
dismantling and
reassembly of the temples
of Philae. *(Photo: Unesco/*
*Laurenza.)*

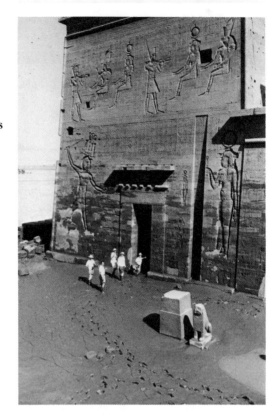

population. This characteristic of the modern temper has evolved
gradually as a result of various forces, including the rise of historicism
and national cultural identities as well as the revulsion against
widespread destructive change.[2]

Unesco has played a major role in channelling this contemporary
need. It has been responsible in particular for nurturing a key idea:
that there is a *world cultural heritage* common to all humanity, an
indivisible whole for which there is a shared responsibility. Thus the
World Heritage List, set up under the 1972 Convention on the
Protection of the World Cultural and Natural Heritage, now includes
216 cultural and natural sites (of which 22 are in the United States
and Canada). It is not simply a roll of honour; the World Heritage
Fund, set up under the same convention, actively supports concrete
conservation projects and meets emergency needs. Another well-
known Unesco programme has been dedicated to large-scale inter-

national preservation and fund-raising campaigns. Nineteen have been launched since 1960 and another nine are in varying degrees of preparation. Speakers at the Washington conference have been able to provide detailed information on several of these projects: Abu Simbel and Philae, the first and most spectacular of them all; the temple of Borobudur (Indonesia); the five-thousand-year-old city of Moenjodaro (Pakistan); the historic city of Sana'a (Yemen Arab Republic); the Wadi Hadramawt and city of Shibam (People's Democratic Republic of Yemen); Istanbul and Göreme in Cappadocia (Turkey); the heritage of the Kathmandu Valley (Nepal); the ancient cities of Sri Lanka; citadels and palaces in Haiti; and finally the Paharpur Vihara monastery and the mosque city of Bagerhat (Bangladesh). Yet even all these projects combined add up to no more than a fraction of the preservation activity taking place today.[3]

We can also look at the collision course proposition less literally— as was surely the intention of those who worded it. In this way of thinking modernization is equaled with industrialization and its consequences,[4] particularly urbanization. There can be no doubt that the destruction brought about by such processes has been and continues to be considerable. The urban landscape, in particular, has paid a heavy price, suffering irreparable damage at the hands of architects and town-planners subservient to a purely materialist logic. In the industrialized countries, awareness of such damage is growing, and—parallel to the already strong environmentalist movements— the cause of heritage protection has progressed remarkably. But still more needs to be done.

In the poorer countries of the Southern Hemisphere, on the other hand, many of the errors of past industrialization are being repeated today. In adapting to present-day needs, too many planners and developers seek to recreate the factors to which the success of Europe's industrial revolution is wrongly attributed. The irony of this situation is that technologies are now available that could make it possible to avoid urban concentration and its heavy social and ecological costs (the excesses of which the Scandinavian countries appear to have successfully averted).[5] Thinking people in the industrializing nations are faced with the unpleasant reality that every step towards a certain kind of modernization is fraught with danger. They must combat a logic forcing countries to build gigantic dams that disturb a whole region's ecology, to apply massive quantities of fertilizer that ruin centuries'-old soil, to create industrial plants that pollute wide expanses of the earth, to adopt urban development plans that perpetuate slum living for generations to come, or to unwittingly choose an education

Pagoda roofs,
Kathmandu, Nepal.
Unesco's International
Campaign for the
Safeguarding of the
Kathmandu Valley was
launched in 1979. *(Photo:
Unesco/Cart.)*

that ensures continuing alienation for their people. To accept the challenge of this combat is not to turn our back on technological progress but rather to insist on its humanization and on careful planning in advance. For late twentieth-century technology is much more devastating than its predecessors, and the champions of heritage preservation in the developing countries are fewer in number, poorer, and less effectively organized. This is particularly tragic at the present time when the recovery, strengthening, and projection of a cultural identity—of which the heritage is the prime manifestation—is experienced as a basic need by all.

More care and more careful choices are needed everywhere. It would be beyond our means here to go more deeply into the heavy costs of modernization. Many of these costs will be analyzed better by other contributors, whose practical field experience enables them to give specific focus to these generalizations. But some of the particularly negative aspects can be described briefly.

Uncontrolled urban growth clearly causes irrevocable damage, but planned development too—theoretically "modern"—has often done no more than superimpose inadequate regulations on an old urban

Polonnaruwa, Sri Lanka. The magnificent recumbent Buddha carved out of the rock face at this ancient Sri Lankan capital. Unesco's International Campaign for the Safeguarding of the Cultural Triangle of Sri Lanka was launched in 1980. *(Photo: Unesco/Alexis N. Vorontzoff.)*

fabric. Archaeological sites and landscapes have been and continue to be violated by major engineering projects such as dams, highways, etc., and by deep ploughing. Reporting in a recent issue of *Museum*, American underwater archaeologist Robert F. Marx described destructive practices from around the world and declared that "the most challenging problem confronting all archaeology is the accelerating pace at which sites are being destroyed. As bulldozers scar millions of hectares each year and whole valleys are inundated for reservoirs and recreational lakes, irreplaceable opportunities to unravel and illuminate the past are lost. Man is indeed earth's most destructive force, but until recently most of his depredations were confined to the land. Today, however, he dredges and fills, floods, pollutes and plunders. Although scuba divers are responsible for looting and destroying many underwater sites of archaeological significance, a greater number are actually ruined by dredging and landfill operations. In fact, this problem is so grave that literally hundreds of shipwrecks are being lost every year and yet no outcry has been uttered either by archaeologists or the public"[6] Marx also condemned vandals and looters, both professional and nonprofessional, whose

activity has been made possible by other concomitants of progress—
shrinking distances and mass tourism. New technology has hastened
the disappearance of traditional skills, forcing the craftsman out of
existence; like the English poet A. E. Housman, he is "a stranger and
afraid, in a world [he] never made."[7]

Air pollution everywhere is eating away masonry and stone, especially limestones such as marble, which had survived intact for
centuries. New materials—"miracle products" such as reinforced
concrete, plastic resins, etc.—have caused secondary reactions that
have accelerated deterioration.[8] Modernization of military technology,
and the scale of its application, have made the horror of indiscriminate
destruction even more massive in time of war.

In terms of material effects, then, modernization as industrialization
is preservation's main enemy. But this is certainly not true for all its
effects. Natural decay continues, but science and technology make it
every day easier to contain. The educational effects of modernization
have also brought about increased awareness of the conservation
rationale, not enough by any means, but sufficiently to reduce neglect
and indifference.

There is also one particularly insidious, apparently nondestructive
effect of what passes for international modernism: standardization in
the built, visual, and daily environment. The specific cultural characteristics of all peoples—their cultural identities—are severely threatened by an advancing tide of uniformity. Inherited cultural values as
a whole, in both their tangible and intangible forms, are subjected to
this onslaught. Strong reactions to it can be observed everywhere, not
just in developing countries.

Those who seek to turn away from a standardized culture are
neither rejecting the present nor taking refuge in the past—which in
any case can only be recreated. They stand for neither regression nor
stagnation. They are motivated by the conviction that an alternative
future is possible.

This brings us back to the first interpretation of our proposition.
Responding to the demands of a rapidly changing world makes
heritage preservation more necessary, not less. This has been clearly
and frequently stated as one of the essential tenets of Unesco's
international work; it is a principle subscribed to by the representatives
and conservationists of *all* countries, regardless of their degree of
"development." In both word and deed, the experience of each
country demonstrates that the inspiration and guidance of its own
cultural traditions are indispensable for an authentic, original approach to the creation of a better future. That future depends as

much on mastery of science and technology as on creative reappropriation of the historical and cultural heritage. And the argument is not rooted in sentiment alone. Using the heritage is often a *practical* solution to problems: it can be cheaper, and both materials and skills may be more readily available.

In the richer countries conflicts of interest certainly remain, for example, between the imperatives of preservation and those of better housing. Yet a look at American cities, where the fabric of one "inner city" after another is being rehabilitated for use today, will show us how powerful, how popular, and how *rational* on the economic calculus the preservation movement has become. The recycling of the entire Covent Garden area of London is another recent example, and the restoration of the Marais quarter in Paris has also entered the annals of historical preservation.

The rapidly expanding desire to preserve the past—motivated largely by a reaction to the pace at which modern technology destroys and outpaces even itself—also contains the seeds of a new danger. Where should we draw the line when every manifestation of the creativity of the past is held up for protection? How do we choose? Yet precisely because modern societies are able to organize safeguard activities in a coherent way, armed with increasingly complete inventories, laws, policies, public or private administrative infrastructures, trained personnel, and perhaps most important of all, a broad base of popular commitment among their citizenry, the grounds for optimism are more than reasonable.

In the poorer countries, however, a true conservation ethic still struggles to exist. That struggle is to be lost or won "in the minds of men." Too many people still view development as a single end product—a state of urban, industrial affluence backed by capital-intensive technology. Even today, despite all the damage, waste, and inequity engendered by this model, the drive to catch up with the more "developed" Joneses survives stubbornly, with sad consequences for architecture and town-planning.

The phenomenon is particularly unsettling to conservators concerned with the integrity of the Arabo-Islamic city, whose identity is so strong. A recent article in the journal *South*, for example, describes the efforts of pioneers such as Hasan Fathy (Egypt) and Mohamed Makiya (Iraq) to turn back the amorphous tide of international modernism by educating a new generation of architects in their own traditions of building and design. The author of the article stresses that "responsibility, respect, intent are words that figure large in Makiya's discourse" and quotes him as saying "intent is at the heart of the architect's design. He must keep on coming back to examine this and keep it clear. If not, his work becomes empty and arrogant. The purpose of architecture is to create an environment or improve on it—at least not to damage what is already there. The architect frames the living space and patterns of people: he provides something fitting for their beliefs, aspirations and needs."⁹ The argument holds, mutatis mutandis, for the preservation and adaptive reuse of old buildings as well.

Other contributors will give flesh and blood to this argument. It is the basis of their professional activity within the network of international cooperation that functions under the aegis of Unesco. Thanks to the determination of men and women such as they, we know that the search for a modern identity is being carried out less and less at the expense of the heritage of the past. Damage is being halted and neglect overcome as the notion of safeguard gradually takes root and contemporary uses of the heritage are developed. A considerable reservoir of traditional models and skills still exists (the latter have almost completely died out in industrialized countries of the Northern Hemisphere) and is being used to restore confidence in indigenous cultural values.

But the needs vastly outstrip the means available—funds, frameworks, and specialized expertise. It would be irresponsible to talk about heritage conservation alone, as if scarce resources were not, in many cases, urgently needed elsewhere. Hence the importance of the *organizational* concomitants of modernization. Heritage conservation today—because of the multiple demands of economic and urban growth—is necessarily complex, requiring an interweave of disciplines and decision-making. This integration of approaches can only be achieved through a national conservation policy—defined and coordinated by the state but calling upon private and individual energies as well—based upon concerted efforts at the highest level among the authorities responsible for cultural affairs, planning and finance, economic and social development, the environment, tourism, etc. The thrust of Unesco's work can be easily understood in relation to a modernization process described in these terms. Whether it is *operational* (concrete safeguard projects on the ground and across the world), *normative* (international conventions that embody standards defined for the world community, based on a synthesis of already successful national legislation that can serve as a model for new legislation in other countries), or *scientific and technical* (study projects whose results contribute to improving professional knowledge and practice), the organization's cultural heritage programme is designed to help forge a coherent approach. International cooperation is thus brought to bear on the following areas: identifying and understanding the heritage (inventories and studies); giving it legal protection; mobilizing funds and organizing better management of funds; training specialized personnel; and promoting public awareness.

Adequate legislation is the basic tool for implementing any global policy. Over the last three decades many states—advised by Unesco among others—have adopted new legislation for this purpose or have strengthened existing laws. Nonetheless, the countries that possess adequate legal protection for their heritage are still exceptions. So too are those whose legislation requires completing detailed inventories of movable and immovable cultural property. The absence of this essential tool makes even the best legislation a dead letter.

Good management—a rarity even in the most industrially advanced countries when it comes to the administration of the arts and cultural affairs—is another feature of modernization that can only work in favour of heritage preservation. So too is a better educational system, one capable of training the skilled craftspersons, engineers, architects, and professionals who can get the most mileage out of what will never be more than a tiny share of the national budget.

Voluntary commitment, funds, and energies are indispensable. This means educating the public in the philosophy of heritage conservation and enlisting its aid. It means building pride and responsibility. In recent years the mushrooming of heritage associations, citizens' groups, youth initiatives, and the like has provided the underpinning to the heritage "boom" in much of Europe and North America. A growing body of experience shows that, despite all the obstacles, a similar awareness is taking root elsewhere.[10]

The preservation of cultural identity is far from being a mere figure of rhetoric. Creative interaction with the past offers a new series of opportunities rather than a string of constraints. There are now many thousands of men and women throughout the world who are dedicated to fulfilling these opportunities. They would have no problem agreeing with the quotation that headed this paper.

*Notes*

1. Amadou-Mahtar M'Bow, Introduction to *Thinking Ahead: Unesco and the Challenges of Today and Tomorrow* (Paris, 1977).

2. This argument is neatly summarized in David Lowenthal and Marcus Binney, eds., *Our Past Before Us. Why do we save it?* (London: Temple Smith, 1981), 19: "Preservation interests have proliferated in our own time largely because these forces have all intensified. Resurgent tribal and local loyalties

require the reaffirmation of symbolic links with the material past. Psychology and psychoanalysis emphasize the significance of links with our personal past. And the pace of technological change, the radical modernization of the built environment, the speed of material obsolescence, an increasing propensity to migrate to new homes, and greater longevity combine to leave us in ever less familiar environments; we are remote even from our own recently remembered past. In a world grown so strange, we hunger for the sense of permanence that tangible relics can best provide. Prevailing doubts—disaffection with modern structures, pessimism about the future—add fuel to nostalgia for the past, which has so lengthened and deepened that we now treasure and preserve the remains of the everyday and the familiar, along with the monumental and magnificent relics, of all epochs."

3. To do full justice to cultural heritage preservation would require an analysis of museums and the preservation of *movable* cultural property. Yet apart from the fact that this conference focuses on the preservation of the *immovable* cultural heritage—monuments and sites—the key issues in the museum world today are essentially different in nature from the problems raised here.

4. The *Fontana Dictionary of Modern Thought* (1977) explains that modernization is a term used by scholars such as S. N. Eisenstadt and W. W. Rostow for "all developments in modern societies which follow in the wake of *industrialization* and *mechanization*" (emphasis added).

5. Georges Corm, "Economic Possibilities and Income Distribution in the Arab Countries: Their Effect on Education and Job Opportunities" in *Population Education and Development in the Arab Countries* (Beirut: Unesco 1977).

6. Robert F. Marx, "The Disappearing Underwater Heritage," *Museum* (Unesco), no. 137 [also catalogued as Vol. 35, no. 1] 1983.

7. Quoted by Lewis Mumford in his *The Conduct of Life* (New York: Harcourt Brace Jovanovich, 1970).

8. In an editorial entitled "A Challenge to the Professions," *Museum* (Unesco) 34, no. 1 (1982), Gaël de Guichen lists a rising tide of dangers to both immovable and movable cultural property.

9. Judith Vidal-Hall, "In Search of Identity—Past into Present," *South,* no. 40 (February 1984).

10. A particularly striking example is the mushrooming success of India's new National Trust for Art and Cultural Heritage (INTACH).

# Preservation versus Modernization
## Realities in Islamic Architecture

RONALD LEWCOCK

The clash between the aims of cultural preservation and the desire for modernization has become a serious issue in light of the steadily diminishing residues of heritage, particularly in urban areas, and an increasing rejection of traditional values by many classes of society. The effects of these clashes are now at their most severe in Africa and Asia, where until recently the pace of modernization was slow and the strength of conservation high. The last decade has seen a marked change in that situation, a change I have been particularly concerned with as a consultant in architectural and urban conservation and rehabilitation in the Islamic countries of the Middle East.

Contemporary city administrators and regional and urban planners in the Middle East are loathe to become involved in cultural preservation or the adaptive reuse of old buildings, neighbourhoods, or city centres: the administrators because the patterns of land ownership, rehousing, fixed rents, and the political ramifications among the people are often daunting; the planners because almost all their training is in the provision of new suburbs or new towns on virgin sites—they have practically no conceptual training in ways of improving existing urban fabrics of old types. Indeed the gulf between the utopian ideologies of the new planners and the practical commonsense fabrics that have evolved over centuries is extreme. Most planners simply do not know how to make the adjustment; they are unable to perceive, or unwilling to admit, the very real values inherent in traditional patterns.

On a practical level, both the politicians and the planners would generally prefer to clear an area in order to begin anew without all the attendant problems, complexities, and unfamiliarities that urban and building conservation involve.

But total clearing of an area itself entails political repercussions.

Sometimes, to avoid these, the politicians and the planners are content
with road widening or, even worse, with driving wide roads through
traditional areas. Where individual buildings are thought to be of
particular value they may be moved out of the way in their entirety
(for example, the beautiful fourteenth-century mosque opposite Bab
Zuwayla in Cairo); more often the building is truncated so that a
range of its rooms simply disappears completely, and the façade is
rebuilt near the centre of its original plan. Where repairs are done
at all to the monuments, public buildings, or houses affected by the
road widening, the façades are moved back—or worse, inferior
makeshift facades replace the original ones.

The effect of such wide roads on the traditional fabric is generally
catastrophic. The intimacy of the spaces in old cities was a reflection
of the ease of interaction among its people, something which is
unthinkable, let alone practicable, across wide roads filled with fast-
moving traffic or through areas of parked cars. Furthermore, the
relatively narrow streets of traditional cities in hot climates ensured
that they were in shade for a large part of each day, and therefore
neither the people nor the buildings were exposed to the sun. Narrow
sidestreets provided secluded, semiprivate access spaces to neighbourhoods, which facilitated a sense of community and the enjoyment
of life. With the intrusion of the motorcar, these lanes have become
blocked, impassable and alien. Widening them, or knocking down
buildings to provide parking spaces off them, does nothing to restore
the communal seclusion and cohesion.

In such developments, monuments become isolated instead of part
of a continuous urban fabric. Indeed one of the characteristics of
modernization is a policy of deliberately, or faute de mieux, isolating
monuments that are not meant to be seen in isolation. The sea of
parked cars around them is often the coup de grace to their original
character.

There are also technical problems introduced by modernization.
Apart from pollution from noxious gases produced by industry and
vehicle exhausts, which accelerate the decay of building surfaces at
an extraordinarily rapid rate, there are other alarming effects introduced by the modernization of the urban environment.

One of the most visible of the technical problems, as well as one of
the most serious, is the extent to which dampness is rising to
unprecedented levels in the buildings. The reason for this development can be stated very simply: in each rapidly growing city, as the
population density has gone up, water has been made available to
more people in much greater quantities than ever before; but the

infrastructure for draining that water out of the area of the city has usually not been supplied, or, if it has, it has not been adequate in size or standard.

The water draining into the ground seems to be lifting the water table up to the point at which it causes damage to the buildings. In many cases the water table is actually coming out at ground level, as the pools continually lying in the streets testify.

Water rising in the walls causes tremendous damage of course; add the fact that it is polluted water and the problems increase. This is clearly, then, a major problem that must be solved in conserving buildings or rehabilitating an old area, because the cost of rectifying it represents something like a quarter to a third of the total cost of any conservation or rehabilitation program.

Shibam in Democratic Yemen has the highest mud buildings that we know of in the world; some of its houses are over a hundred feet high. But the very inadequate drainage systems are bringing the sewage down into the streets and straight into the ground. Again the contamination of the water in the ground from sewage and other factors has produced extraordinary problems. Cracking may begin in one corner of a building at the bottom, and by the time it reaches the sixth floor it runs through the whole structure in every direction— these are major cracks, an inch and a half or two inches across.

Sanaa has high buildings, too, and the introduction of a piped water supply has caused more problems than it has resolved. As in the case of many Third World cities, the piped water system was introduced without any complementary piped drainage system—the old city of Sanaa still has no communal drains. The Minister of Water told me that in the last eighteen months he has paid just under a million American dollars in compensation for about forty collapsed houses in the old city.

Electricity is another kind of modern convenience that is ruining old cities and the appearance of buildings in a number of ways. The wires are simply festooned across the walls or form spiderwebs at the tops of leaning poles in the narrow streets.

Another problem is traffic circulation. By now the number of motorized vehicles has so increased and so tyrannized pedestrians that the market streets have become unpleasant indeed. Cars and trucks are parked everywhere and block the passages. This raises the major issue of whether one can allow such a situation to continue. Is it logical to allow modernization to take place so that one can insist on segregation? The municipality in Sanaa is agonizing over this question at the moment. They have tentatively decided to restrict

View from a house overlooking the Great Mosque, Shibam, showing the damage done to the parapet of the mud-brick house by rain after a few years of neglect.

traffic to a very limited number of streets in the old city, to segregate pedestrians from motorized traffic, and to limit the access of vehicles to restricted times at night. But whether these policies are enforceable is another matter.

Deterioration from lack of maintenance is yet another major concern. Buildings constructed in the traditional ways in the Islamic world were meant to be maintained. It was an accepted part of life that, after the rains, repainting and replastering would be needed to repair any water damage, for if this was not done every year deterioration was extraordinarily rapid. Now annual maintenance is no longer an accepted part of life, and the consequences are severe. First the roofs go, then the corners fall off because the walls have been damaged by the rains. In no time at all fairly respectable multistoried buildings have become ruined single-storey structures. They are left as single-storey buildings and not allowed to collapse entirely because shopkeepers and craftspersons occupy the ground floor, and the rent they pay in most traditional societies, whether rent-controlled or not, represents the bulk of the profit on a building investment. It is therefore in everyone's interest, including the owners', to maintain the ground floors. They waterproof the floors of what were once the first storeys (i.e., the ceilings of the ground floor), and they become the roofs of the buildings.

Nor is this limited to unprofitable rental buildings, where decaying structures can be attributed to the grasping mentality of landlords who allow their buildings to decay because the rents are too low. It is happening to some of the major monuments of Islam. In Cairo probably 30 percent of the *waqf* properties in the old city are shrinking storey by storey; some have already reached the groundfloor level, with ghostly walls rising up three or four floors. In one *waqf* property in Cairo, the canvas-makers' suq near the Bab Zuwayla, the upper levels of the suq, once beautifully designed and comfortable *waqf* houses, have all been allowed to decay. Yet this suq has always been regarded by everybody concerned with conservation in Cairo as one of the major monuments. We must come to terms with the principle of annual maintenance if we are going to talk about preserving and upgrading Islamic cities.

Natural disasters also pose more than just the obvious conservation problems; we tend to think only of immediate problems and ignore potential ones. In many areas of the Middle East, for example, flooding is frequent but not usually very serious; it can be controlled with diversion dams. Once every thirty, fifty, or hundred years, however, a major flood occurs. Everybody knows there will be one because the city has been washed away regularly once or twice a century for a thousand years. Nobody does anything about it, however, and one of the first priorities of any conservation scheme should be to take steps to anticipate the problem. Similarly, although there has not been a major earthquake for a long time, history tells us that major earthquakes are possible all through the Middle East. Conservation efforts need to anticipate this possibility as well.

In a recent flood in Shibam, not only the city walls but a number of houses behind them collapsed; this raises an allied issue. Land tenure in the Islamic world, as we know, is very different from that in the West. One of the ways it differs is that the people who live immediately behind the city walls were traditionally responsible for the maintenance of the section of wall directly in front of them. Street cleaning was another traditional task of the inhabitants of the abutting houses. These customs have rapidly fallen away in the last twenty years—in some places as recently as in the last six or seven years. In Shibam the inhabitants say, "We're now living in a modern state;

The Shibam city wall, collapsed through neglect and the action of
sewerage water.

we've got a powerful central government; why should we pay for
repairing the town wall?" It is an extraordinary attitude considering
that when the walls fall, the houses behind them crack and eventually
collapse as well.

Ownership, as we know, poses still other problems. Even buildings
regarded as national monuments can be privately owned, and private
ownership can involve so many members of a family that the protection
and maintenance of the monument can be prevented through lack
of agreement or for want of a single person to take responsibility.

Inadequate material for repair produces another problem. A marvellous Islamic material, which most people have forgotten exists, is
called by different names in different places. It is a very hard lime
plaster made by pounding as many as five, six, or seven layers one
after another. This extraordinary technique can also be used for
decoration, although it takes considerable skill. The material has an
amazing life: traditional builders say it lasts for two hundred years,
but it is possible to date existing surfaces back much further. Those
who have been to archaeological sites in the Islamic world will have
seen it on cisterns, both recently excavated and long exposed to
weather, and sometimes demonstrably more than a thousand years
old. The material is extraordinarily strong. Even though it is very

An old *gadad* (decorated plinth) in Sanaa, which, because of careless repair with modern cement, has been damaged by chemical action of the free salts contained in the cement.

hard, it does not crack, because lime expands and contracts with the weather. It has only one drawback: cement cannot be put against it because cement will attack its small gypsum content until it disintegrates. The point illustrates the grave dangers inherent in not understanding the technology one is working with if one is repairing or maintaining traditional buildings.

Another aspect of the annual maintenance problem is that repair of traditional building materials involves techniques requiring a high degree of skill. Building a house of earth nearly a hundred feet high requires a great deal of knowledge about the techniques of mud-brick building. Layered earth is another elaborate technique that involves, among other things, hammering the mud into place with a heavy block of wood for about an hour for each square meter. Given current rates for construction workers in the Middle East, this becomes very costly, and what looks like a cheap material turns out to be a phenomenally expensive one. What can we do about annual maintenance, if repairing these buildings costs so much?

Using traditional materials has all sorts of other ramifications. The hundred-foot-high buildings in Shibam were built with apparently crude bricks of mud with straw reinforcement in them. In the opinion of all the best builders, this mud has to come from around the roots

**Layered mud walls of the old city as they were in 1975.**

of a healthy, strong date palm. If it does not come from the best
arable land, then the building will not be strong. Chemical analysis
shows why: the continual irrigation by flood waters increases the
amount of fine clay in arable land, leaving a higher percentage of
pure clay in this earth than in that taken from a nonagricultural or
a deserted area. It is also relatively free of salt, since continual watering
allows the salt to sink down to a very low level. But removing arable
land for building material comes into direct conflict with attempts to
improve agriculture and is now forbidden by law. What building
materials should be used for maintenance if the traditional sources
are forbidden? Obviously the government ministries need to look for
alternative materials, and we hope they will.

In addition to the problem of annual maintenance, there is, of
course, the question of repair after damage. It can be done, but
modern architects cannot easily tackle it. It too is a very specialized
and skilled business. A layer of mud added onto mud bricks or a
layered mud wall will simply fall off again unless the laborious
techniques of experienced master masons are used to fuse it with the
old wall. In some cases we have yet to find alternative techniques to
repair these buildings that could be employed fairly cheaply. In short
the traditional buildings of much of the Arab world may have been
economical to build and maintain until seven or eight years ago, but
they are rapidly becoming expensive, mainly because of all the manual
work required.

Layered mud walls of the old city photographed in 1982 after years of neglect.

Are there any viable solutions to the problems raised here? To take one example, the waterproofing of existing thick walls in areas where underground, highly corrosive damp is causing major damage to structures can be approached by using a skin on the outside of the walls. The skin can be made of any number of materials that seal in a waterproofing agent, but the technique presumes there is a solid stone foundation underneath the building. In most of the buildings we have been working with, the large foundation stones would hold in the bulk of any fluid. Liquid silicone or stearate can then be gravity-injected to prevent damp from rising into the wall. Membranes have to be introduced on the sides to stop the stearate or the silicone from running out into the soil because the surfaces of these traditional walls are often very porous.

Traditional construction in most Islamic buildings has an outer skin, an inner skin, and a much softer central core. This core is usually a very soft stone that has become pulverized, rather like clay, and it reacts badly with water. It also spills out like a pile of sand if one tries to cut through a wall, making it virtually impossible to put a solid sheet of damp-proofing material through the wall. This necessitates the sort of alternative technique discussed above.

The advanced decay menacing the urban fabric of these cities is of tremendous concern to everyone who admires the extraordinary expression of human achievement represented by Islamic traditional architecture. The situation is symptomatic of that being experienced in every part of the world, in Asia, in India, in China, in Africa, and in Central and South America. The issues are similar and the conflicts and problems are often exactly duplicated. Enormous efforts—marked by clarity of purpose, determination, and the development of specialized technical skills—will be necessary if a significant proportion of the physical cultural wealth of the world is to be preserved for the education and enjoyment of future generations.

# Challenges to Heritage Preservation in Industrially Developed Countries

BERNARD M. FEILDEN

In industrially developed countries, the challenges faced by architectural conservationists fall under six main headings:

*1) the lack of integrated planning and financing on the part of governments;*

*2) the lack of recognition of the skills needed for conservation;*

*3) a shortage of craftsmen and materials;*

*4) the absence of an organisation geared to maintenance in the modern building industry;*

*5) difficulties in quantifying the benefits of conservation; and*

*6) the failure of education to prepare citizens for conservation.*

### Integration

Conservation is a tender plant that needs watering with governmental support and on a continuing basis. It takes over twenty years to set up a fully competent conservation service, and we in Europe are only now beginning to fill the gap caused by the war years and the slow restart that followed.

Well-meaning administrators can either throw more money at you than you can use properly or starve you of the funds needed to finish a project, possibly because of changes in government policy. Governmental standing orders with regard to contract procedure, which may be admirable for a new building, can greatly increase the cost of conservation. But the main cause of escalating costs is undoubtedly stop-go financing.

Administrators have considerable problems with financial control—this certainly requires accountability, but it should not be forgotten that in architectural conservation the historic building is the real client. This is not a plea for architectural licence, for the historic architect has to satisfy much more rigorous critics than others.

Stone carver, York
Minster, England. The
carver is copying a
decayed finial.

In architectural conservation, time is the vital element as decay does not delay while the administration delays making necessary decisions. Delay can cause costs to escalate rapidly. But with clear thinking, objectives and priorities can be defined and the project executed under the control of the designated architect working within a budget previously agreed upon by the administration. For efficiency the cash flow must be steady and the right-size team found to execute the project. It takes a very skilled and experienced administrator to ensure that all this happens—if administrators are good they get promoted and are lost forever to the cause of conservation because of the low priority generally allocated by governments.

At the political level, there is often a conflict of objectives between central and local interests. A town mayor may view an historic building as an impediment to the development of the town centre, while the national interest recognises this building as the sole surviving example of an important architect. Landowners have not been educated to view such a monument as an asset. Were this not so, Sir Christopher Wren's Temple Bar could have been saved long ago.

**Clock Tower, The Square of the October Revolution, Montenegro, Yugoslavia. Repairing damage after an earthquake places great demands on administrative, professional, and craft skills.**

## Skills

Except in the fine arts, the skills of conservationists are not properly recognized. As a result these skills are not paid for either. We may be convinced that our advice will save real values in cultural property, but to the owner who follows our advice the professional fee is real and the savings imaginary. We suffer from this disadvantage and gain nothing by saying "I told you so" when advice is not followed and a predictable disaster occurs.

Part of the trouble is that conservationists are so interested in their work that they are afraid to charge the same rates as a plumber. They also lack continuity and security of employment. More fundamental, however, is the fact that conservationists belong fully neither to science nor to art nor to craft; we are hybrids who do not fit into well-defined patterns. This problem affects government because most administrators are unhappy dealing with artistic matters and tend to look on craftspersons as a lesser order than, say, intellectuals. The scientist, of course, earns respect, but conservators are only *applied* scientists and there is no great commercial spin-off in solving their unique problems.

The American Advisory Council for Historic Preservation has done invaluable work in studying the problems of heritage conservators and in proposing solutions. Conservation needs a central, caring body to represent its justified interests. The need for a multidisciplinary approach is not always appreciated, even by conservationists. When analysing errors, however, one finds that, for example, a town-planner forgot to consult an archaeologist and a landscape architect, or that an architect failed to get art-historical advice. Consultation and getting second and even third opinions is accepted as normal practice in medicine; we must persuade the public that this is desirable and necessary in conservation. Architectural conservation is too serious a business to leave to the judgement of one person. There must be collaboration. In particular, architectural historians must be brought in to perform a responsible role in the understanding of the ethics and economics of conservation.

The historic architect in developed countries faces a severe shortage of craftspersons and traditional material. For example, metrication has slightly altered the sizes of all standard bricks in the United Kingdom. Traditionally there were many sizes of bricks, usually fired in kilns close to the building site and made of local clays. Nowadays a hoped-for match has to be found and transported hundreds of miles. Because such bricks are made of different clays, they will never weather in the same way. Yet because they are a special size these bricks are sold at a high price.

Both local brick kilns and lime kilns have disappeared. In the United Kingdom hydraulic limes are no longer produced and sold, so we have to look to France. There has been a great failure to appreciate the merits of lime mortars, mainly because of the aggressive marketing of Portland cements whose qualities may appeal to the local builder but certainly not to the lover of historic buildings. The use of Portland cement has indeed done more damage to the historic building from the Acropolis on down than any other factor. The local builder likes it because it is quick to set and very strong, and if no architect is involved the building's owner is apt to believe in an honest and practical person. Yet unless it is used properly Portland cement is one of the worst enemies of historic buildings. The wrong use of Portland cement highlights one of the major problems that the conservationist has to face.

Lime mortars, with a possualanic additive, are quite different. They

**Drilling for grout injection, York Minster, England. Drilling is one of the new skills required for the conservation of historic buildings that enables reinforcement and grout to be inserted. Shots up to 21 metres in length were achieved with this equipment, but great care is needed to aim the drill.** *(Photo: Shepherd Building Group.)*

are durable and can become very hard in time, but when newly laid are flexible because of their slow setting characteristics. When set they also have the admirable characteristic of sealing any cracks that may have occurred. Science has to contribute substantial research before we fully understand the complex nature of lime mortars. The problem is considerable for each different limestone produces a different burnt lime. The 1982 report of the American National Materials Advisory Board on the Conservation of Historic Stone Buildings is a valuable contribution to understanding this complex problem.

The tragedy of the modern building industry is that it has discarded so many traditional materials and practices without fully understanding their working significance and compatibility in the totality of an historic building.

Owing to the industrialisation of building we are now short of many materials including wrought iron, crown glass, and oil-based paints, to name only a few. The introduction of resin-based or latex paints has also had disastrous effects on some historic buildings. The pigments used are different and often based on dyes, and the dispersion is much more regular, hence robbing paint of its interest. The medium has been changed from oil to a durable resin, making maintenance much more difficult. The paint does not reduce to a powdery surface but cracks and peels, making subsequent work impossible unless one starts again. The aim of industry is to produce "maintenance free" products, but this means, rather, that these products are simply impossible to maintain. The essential aspect of historic buildings is that they were designed to be maintained.

Industrialisation has brought many more problems to the historic building conservator than those I have mentioned. For instance, virgin forests have been consumed and no substitutes can be found for the timbers that are needed to restore some of our historic buildings. Six oak trees, some 17 m long and 46 by 54 cm square, were needed to reconstruct the roof of York Minster, but only one such beam could be found in the United Kingdom. It is essential that some forests of fine timber should be set aside for future conservation work.

Industrialisation has also almost priced artisans out of existence. I realize that this raises a complex social problem; but if one wants to keep craftspersons for conservation, they should be paid a wage somewhat above the industrial average. This is done in Poland, where it was realised that a programme of architectural conservation was vital to the survival of the nation after the catastrophes of World War II. Poland's PKZ organisation engaged over 9,000 artisans earning more than the industrial wage and some 2,500 professionals with university training in a comprehensive programme. Conservation was a vital element in the natural regeneration of Poland. If relatively poor nations can do this, why can the richer nations not do better?

Apart from Japan, which since 1929 has classified master craftspersons as a "living cultural heritage," no developed country has taken sufficient measures to preserve the knowledge held by craftspersons. Much of this knowledge cannot be communicated by writing or analyzed by scientists. It can only be handed down from master to apprentice.

Unfortunately, developed countries have superseded this system by an academic approach. However, the wheel of time continues to turn. In India a craftsman's three sons became an administrator, a doctor, and a lawyer, whereas in Holland the fathers of young conservators in training were doctors, lawyers, and administrators.

The central boss in the central tower, York Minster, England. Cleaning revealed St. Peter and St. Paul, but the latter lacks his sword. Traces of ancient colour must be sought and traditional pigments used for restoration. This work demands special skills and should be done by a conservator. *(Photo: Shepherd Building Group.)*

Developed countries are just beginning to value craftspersons—perhaps because of their scarcity.

Without craftspersons, the historic architect is nothing. Artisans will not survive unless they are properly paid and given due status and a continuity of work. Without them we will have eaten the seed corn of the future—a course of action that would result in a cultural famine.

It is evident that technical changes in the building industry have resulted in a decline in the demand for skilled craftspersons. With off-site construction of some elements, the industry has wanted workers who can assemble prefabricated units, and this has reduced a whole range of specialist trades to wet and dry operatives. Bonus schemes have tended to pay for muscle not skill, thus producing low standards of workmanship. Anything requiring time and skill tends to be considered prohibitively expensive. Ironically, the skilled older workers are given difficult finishing jobs and are paid less than the muscular operatives. These skilled craftspersons are getting on in age and have not been replaced. We are losing their expertise, and the problem is how to replace what we have lost—how can we emulate the plasterwork and decorative arts of the Renaissance and the baroque period or even of the neoclassical and Victorian eras?

The Council of Europe has recognised the problem of training by setting up a small centre on the island of San Servolo near Venice where short specialist courses are given to forty craftspersons a year.

## Maintenance

The shortage of suitable craftspersons and building firms for the maintenance of historic buildings is making the architect's job increasingly difficult. Architects have to know more about the craftsperson's job and techniques in order to get good workmanship even at a quite ordinary level. In the preindustrial period, maintenance was a normal routine because the techniques of building and repair were virtually the same. Nowadays there is no such similarity, and maintenance has to be studied scientifically. Architects in developed countries are largely unaware of the maintenance factor when making new designs. Maintenance is usually left to the so-called practical men who do not understand the nature of historic buildings and rashly use incompatible materials. Any new material must be carefully tested before it is used on a large scale in an historic building; in fact it is wise to use only traditional materials unless they are proven to have failed.

The building industry has not been able to organise maintenance of property and this has caused untold inconvenience to its public. In Holland, however, there is a scheme, partly subsidised by the government, for annual inspections of historic buildings by qualified architects. This has been successful in initiating a policy of preventive maintenance. Over the past twenty-five years the Church of England has also run a quinquennial inspection scheme that has prevented many mediæval buildings from collapse and greatly reduced the cost of caring for this rich heritage.

## Costs and Benefits

It is an illusion to think that conservation is always costly. In fact, if introduced early enough into the planning or execution of projects, conservation can save large sums of money. At Chesterfield in the United Kingdom, for example, it was shown that existing buildings could be rehabilitated at two-thirds of the cost of building new edifices in the same area, with additional savings on the infrastructure or roads, sewers, and services. This scheme was awarded the Europa Nostra Silver Medal in 1982.

But rising standards and ever more severe building regulations inhibit the rehabilitation of much of our urban fabric. Governments give grants to assist conservation of historic buildings, but often the rules are too complicated, the inspectors too slow, and the terms even distasteful to the owner of the property. By charging value-added tax on repairs to historic buildings, governments also take away with one hand what they give with the other. The tax relief given to owners of historic buildings in the United States is a far more effective way of stimulating conservation, especially since it is controlled by exemplary standards and guidelines.

## Education

Perhaps the most fundamental challenge, however, relates to education. Children are taught to be "numerate" and "literate" and to read poems and novels; but they are not taught to see and understand what they look at. When children can read the elevation of a building like a poem, or a street like a novel, we will get true environmental consciousness. Today's children will be tomorrow's citizens. If they leave their own towns a little better than they found them, they will have fulfilled their duty to posterity. The challenge for us is to do our duty by them.

# Mobilizing
# Resources
# for Preservation

# International Assistance for the Conservation of Cultural Property

HIROSHI DAIFUKU

The twentieth century has been a period of turmoil and change. Some of us in the industrialized nations, confronted with the problems and adjustments required by change, undoubtedly look upon the past with nostalgia. [Preservation is equated with a romanticized past, a period of stability and plenty. Others are concerned with the maintenance of tradition, while still others look upon preservation programmes as elitist. They prefer to look towards the future in the belief the future will mean improvement in their social and economic status.

These diverging points of view are also found among developing countries. Some look upon conservation as a means of maintaining continuity with the past; the need is felt even more strongly than in the developed countries, as the contrast between a simpler folk society and the current trend to large urban populations presents marked contrasts between the well-to-do and the poor who live in slums. Some, however, view preservation movements as neocolonial attempts—at best well-meaning interference—by outsiders who would like to keep the poor as they are and to deny them modern technology.

Nevertheless, in spite of these diverging points of view there is clear evidence that interest in the conservation of cultural property is growing throughout the world. In part this has been due to the reaction against the anonymity and the dehumanizing effects of large urban conglomerations, the spread of international styles in architectural design, and the standardization of mass-produced products. In spite of conflicting priorities, it is surprising to see how many have committed themselves to major conservation programmes.

### Restoration and the Rise of International Standards

For centuries it has been the practice to continue to use old buildings, and additions were made or repairs undertaken on a more or less haphazard basis. In some countries a religious structure was maintained with little or no change, or rebuilt at fixed intervals with the replacement faithfully replicating the old. Usually, however, changes were made reflecting different trends in styles or taste, so that a building of any size might have a number of anachronistic elements. This situation still prevails in all but a few cases in which historic authenticity has become an ideal.

It was not until the nineteenth and twentieth centuries that conservation principles were first developed. An early theory was that of Viollet-le-Duc (1814–1879), who believed it was important not only to define the history of a building but to return it to its original character. In other words, the architect should determine the period of the greatest perfection of a monument. Its restoration would then include the removal of elements detracting from this ideal. Another school of thought argued against restoration, considering ruins objects of beauty in their own right.

With the development of the scientific method and its influence on historic research, a further evolution took place. Historical accuracy and authenticity became an ideal, and previous changes—unless they were poor—were kept as part of the historic background when restoration was required.

During the period between the two world wars, the League of Nations established the International Institute for Intellectual Cooperation (IIIC) in Paris. It had, among its bureaus, the International Office of Museums (IOM). One of the projects of the IOM was to bring together leading experts in the fields of conservation and restoration of monuments and sites to resolve differences and to arrive at internationally accepted principles. This resulted in 1931 in the formulation and adoption of the Athens Charter, which was used by the National Park Service in the United States, among other institutions and professionals.

When Unesco was founded in the aftermath of World War II, it took over many of the projects that had been carried out by the IIIC. Thus the second paragraph of Article I of the Unesco constitution states that it will

> *(c) Maintain, increase and diffuse knowledge; By assuring* (inter
> alia) *the conservation and protection of the world's inheritance of books,*

*works of art and monuments of history and science, and recommending to the nations concerned the necessary international conventions.*

In 1954 the General Conference of Unesco adopted an international convention on the Protection of Cultural Property in the Event of Armed Conflict, also known as the Hague Convention. It defined cultural property as

(a) *movable or immovable property of great importance to the cultural heritage of every people, such as monuments of architecture, art or history, whether religious or secular; archaeological sites; groups of buildings which, as a whole, are of historical or artistic interest; works of art; manuscripts, books and other objects of artistic, historical or archaeological interest; as well as scientific collections and important collections of books or archives or of reproductions of the property defined above;*

(b) *buildings whose main effective purpose is to preserve or exhibit the movable property defined in sub-paragraph (a) such as museums, large libraries and depositories of archives, and refuges intended to shelter, in the event of armed conflict, the movable property defined in subparagraph (a) and (b), to be known as "centers containing monuments."*

Since then two other conventions have been adopted, both ratified by the American government: on the Means of Prohibiting and Preventing the Illicit Import, Export and Transfer of Ownership of Cultural Property (1970) and concerning the Protection of the World Cultural and Natural Heritage, also known as the World Heritage Convention (1972).

The General Conference has also adopted international *recommendations* on International Principles Applicable to Archaeological Excavations (1956); concerning the Most Effective Means of Rendering Museums Accessible to Everyone (1960); concerning the Safeguarding of the Beauty and Character of Landscapes and Sites (1962); on the Means of Prohibiting and Preventing the Illicit Export, Import and Transfer of Ownership of Cultural Property (1964); concerning the Preservation of Cultural Property Endangered by Public or Private Works (1968); concerning the Protection at National Level, of the Cultural and Natural Heritage (1972); concerning the Safeguarding and Contemporary Role of Historic Areas (1976); on the International Exchange of Cultural Property (1976); on the Protection of Movable Cultural Property (1978); and for the Safeguarding and Preservation of Moving Images (1980).

Unlike the conventions, these recommendations are not binding on countries that ratify them, but provide recognized and useful standards. The recommendation on archaeological excavations, for example, has been particularly useful as a basis for the preparation of new national legislation by a number of recently independent states.

The problem of standards to be observed in the repair and restoration of monuments was particularly acute following World War II. Mass destruction—particularly due to aerial bombardments that destroyed or severely damaged the historic centres of many cities— was accompanied by shortages of trained personnel and competing priorities for funds, equipment, and supplies. Many makeshift repairs and the hasty acceptance of "miracle products" resulted in restoration work that had to be completely redone at a later date. These factors caused a change in emphasis from the standards set in the Athens Charter. In 1964, at an international congress in Venice, Italy, problems of reconstruction were reviewed. While the Venice Charter is concerned with conservation problems, it accepted a wider definition, than that implied by the term "monuments," in adopting the concept of "cultural property." Thus it took into account the "urban or rural setting in which is found the evidence of a particular civilization." Unesco's later recommendations expanded on some of the themes covered in the Venice Charter.

### Financing the Conservation of Cultural Property

While Unesco immediately provided a channel through which international standards could be established and diffused, in its early years it was unable to provide practical assistance. The General Conference adopted a resolution in 1950 to have a study prepared on the possibility of setting up an international fund that would be financed through a special tax on tourists, either to be added to visa fees or to be paid at airports. The resolution was rejected, however, as it ran counter to the tendency to liberalize travel formalities. In 1952 the government of Switzerland suggested that instead of a fund it would be useful to have an international centre that would coordinate research and eliminate costly duplication of studies, collect and make the appropriate documentation available internationally, and contribute to the training of specialists. This proposal was approved by the sixth session of the General Conference of Unesco and resulted in the establishment, in 1959, of the International Centre for the Study of the

Preservation and the Restoration of Cultural Property in Rome (ICCROM), Italy.

## The Participation Programme

It was also felt, however, that the work of Unesco should not be confined to theoretical problems or to the diffusion of standards. The idea that Unesco should take part in concrete activities carried out at a national or regional level led to the creation in 1955 of a "programme of participation in the activities of Member States," whereby the organization could provide consultants, fellowships, specialized equipment and supplies, and in some cases cash grants to projects that paralleled Unesco's own programme as approved by the General Conference.

For 1955–56 the first appropriation for the preservation of cultural property amounted to only $25,000 out of a total of $1,099,330. "PP," as the Participation Programme came to be known, proved to be very popular. Requests for cultural projects were particularly numerous because other multilateral or bilateral assistance programmes concentrated on economic development, and little assistance was forthcoming for cultural projects. By 1981–83 Unesco's total PP budget amounted to over $15 million, of which over $1 million was spent on heritage conservation projects and the development of museums.

## The International Campaigns

Besides the Participation Programme, the regular programme of Unesco also provides fellowships, consultants, and other forms of assistance for the conservation of the cultural heritage. But these are limited.

During the 1950s the government of Egypt decided that one of the most important projects it would undertake was the construction of a high dam—to provide hydroelectric power and expand irrigation—upstream from Aswan. The USSR agreed to finance its construction. The lake was to have covered much of the valley of the Nile in the Nubian area, from Aswan well into the Sudan. The area to be flooded was, compared with lower Egypt, not well known, although many outstanding monuments of the Pharaonic period were there, particularly the temples of Abu Simbel (built by Rameses II, ca. 1304–1237 B.C.). In December 1959, at the request of the governments of Egypt and the Sudan, the Director-General of Unesco decided to launch an appeal to carry out a programme of archaeological salvage to preserve

**The Great Temple of Abu Simbel on its new site. The International Campaign for the Safeguard of the Nubian Monuments was launched by Unesco in 1960.** *(Photo: Unesco/Nenadovic.)*

some of the principal monuments that would otherwise have been inundated. The campaign was launched on March 8, 1960. The response was worldwide and many countries and institutions contributed to the campaign. In the case of the United States, President John F. Kennedy informed Congress on April 7, 1961, that the government would participate in the campaign by contributions from PL 480 funds, which would meet local costs of American institutions taking part in the archaeological programme for the safeguarding of the Abu Simbel temples. Later the United States also contributed to the preservation of Philae through the use of PL 480 funds.

The budget required to save Abu Simbel amounted to $42 million, and Philae $30 million. Of this amount the government of Egypt paid about half.

In November 1966 torrential rains flooded much of Italy. Two major historic cities, Florence and Venice, were particularly affected. The immediate problems were much more serious in Florence, where rapidly rising flood waters damaged or destroyed many major works of art and historic manuscripts. The disaster coincided with a session of Unesco's General Conference and, in response to an appeal by the

**Work in progress on the reerection of the Small Temple of Abu Simbel on its new site.** *(Photo: Unesco/Nenadovic.)*

Italian delegation—the scope of damage was far greater than could be met by the efforts of Italian restorers alone—volunteers came from other European countries and North America to help in the rescue and salvage of works of art. ICCROM was particularly helpful, as staff were able to help place volunteers in projects where their skills would be most useful. Examples of immediate assistance provided in this emergency abound. A large autoclave that was about to be delivered to a hospital was modified to use ethylene dioxide gas to sterilize water-soaked manuscripts and prevent the growth of mold, and then sent to the archives in Florence. A large quantity of Japanese handmade paper was flown in to be used as a covering for water-damaged paintings to prevent the loss of painted surfaces from canvases and wooden panels. Many student volunteers, with no particular skills but plenty of goodwill, worked on the conservation of manuscripts under the direction of specialists. A large conservation laboratory and atelier were established at the Fortezza di Basso. Within a period of two to three years, the emergency phase was over and the less severely damaged paintings could be stored under controlled conditions to be treated and restored in due course.

In Venice, however, the flood damage was not the only problem. The very survival of the city required long-term planning and execution of works. After the emergency rescue period was over, an analysis of the threats to the city revealed a number of problems. There was the problem of physical geography: the island of Venice was subsiding steadily. In addition to the great flood of 1966, the Piazza San Marco and other low-lying areas of the city were usually flooded by a foot or more of water two or three times a year. Part of this was due to compression of the subsoil over the course of years, owing to the use of artesian wells. The ability of the lagoon to absorb high water had been reduced by large land-fills, created to provide terrain for industry. Moreover, the construction of ship canals in the lagoon increased the effects of tidal currents. Industry in the nearby mainland also contributed to pollution of the lagoon and the atmosphere.

The concomitant demographic changes meant that much of the population was moving to subsidized modern housing on the nearby mainland instead of staying in the historic city—particularly during the off-season for tourism. Employment was seasonal as many hotels, restaurants, and shops close during the off-season, resulting in reduced opportunities for local residents and an influx of temporary labour during the summer. This was accompanied by fewer social and cultural activities for the permanent population.

Years of neglect had also contributed to the physical deterioration of many of Venice's monuments. The banks of the canals were severely eroded, and many of the secondary canals were filled with stagnant, polluted water.

A combination of these factors caused the great flood of 1966: the diminished ability of the lagoon to absorb high water, the flooding river, and the unusually high tide reinforced by a storm in the Adriatic.

In 1968 Unesco cooperated in the preparation of a card index listing important works of art and an inventory of historic buildings. The phenomena of tidal movements and the dynamics of geophysical fluids were the subject of thirty international meetings. On the basis of these and other studies, the government of Italy adopted a Special Law (No. 171) for the safeguard of Venice and the surrounding area, which authorized a budget amounting to the equivalent of $500 million. A great deal has been accomplished in the intervening period and the island has stopped sinking. Aqueducts have been built and most of the artesian wells closed. New, stringent laws have been adopted to reduce pollution from industry. Domestic heating—using coal—has ended with the transition to the use of electricity or natural gas. A modern sewage system has been built to reduce pollution levels in the lagoon.

The distinguishing feature of the Venice campaign has been, however, the decision of the Italian government not to seek financial contributions from foreign governments, or loans to finance the conservation of the city and its surroundings. Many contributions have been made, however, through private committees or organizations. They have undertaken the restoration of works of art, monuments, churches, and so forth. They include committees from countries or groups as far away as Australia and as close as the Rotary Club of Venice. Six American committees, including some established for Venice alone, have contributed to the programme.

There have been a number of other international campaigns. Publicity for these campaigns has also contributed to the local economy, and in many cases will enable the government to amortize the amount it has spent on conservation programmes through the development of tourism. Another positive contribution has been a strengthened, trained, and suitably equipped national service.

### The United Nations and Other International Funding Organizations

Fortunately the programme for the conservation of the cultural heritage can today call upon other international sources of assistance. Taking into account the dislocations caused by World War II and the needs of many of the less-developed countries, the General Assembly of the United Nations authorized a modest programme of technical assistance in 1946, limited to strictly defined goals, that was designed to provide advice on the transfer of technology. However, it was soon realized that this was insufficient, and not only in terms of budget requirements. The scope of the problems was much vaster than anticipated. Largely illiterate, poverty-stricken populations were unable to absorb industrial technology. Disease and malnutrition were also negative factors, and subsistence agriculture could not provide the basis for the development of industry.

The technical assistance programme was reorganized to take into account the need to develop programmes on a broad front, in which different specialized agencies of the United Nations could take part. The programme was retitled Expanded Programme of Technical Assistance (EPTA). EPTA subcontracted work, for example, on agricultural development to the Food and Agricultural Organization (FAO) in Rome; programmes to combat illiteracy and to develop higher education to Unesco; programmes to control malaria and eliminate smallpox to the World Health Organisation (WHO) in Geneva, etc. As the need for capital investment increased, the United Nations established a special United Nations Fund for Economic Development (SUNFED) in 1959. While EPTA and SUNFED had similar goals, they differed in structure and operations. In 1965 the United Nations decided to reduce administrative costs by merging these two units under the title of the United Nations Development Programme (UNDP).

For many years, however, the conservation of cultural property was not considered part of economic development and was therefore ineligible for UNDP financing. It was not until 1969, when the General Assembly of the United Nations adopted a resolution sponsoring an International Year for Tourism, that UNDP was instructed to develop tourism as a contributor to economic development. Historic preservation became eligible thereby for assistance, since monuments are a prime tourist attraction. Once this principle was accepted, it meant a considerable change in the operational programme of Unesco. Up to this point, due to budget limitations all that was possible under the Participation Programme were short-term (two to three weeks, a month or two at most) consultant missions. With UNDP, funding experts could be assigned administrative responsibilities for one to five years. Seconded by local officials, these experts could provide both advice and instruction.

Another aspect of UNDP is the financing of regional projects, in particular for training. This was an important factor in the success of a project that was carried out in Jos, Nigeria, in cooperation with the Nigerian government. During the 1960s, with the decolonization of African states, many African museums lost their European expatriate staff. The project in Jos was designed to train museum technicians in planning and designing modern exhibitions to meet the needs of the local population. The technicians learned printing and photography techniques, among other skills required to operate a modern museum. The need was particularly great as changes were taking place rapidly; unless a fully functioning national museum existed, much of the material would have been sold to collectors from abroad or simply lost. The success of the Jos project led to the establishment of another regional training project in Mexico City as well as one based in Cuzco for the Andean countries in Latin America.

Besides UNDP the World Bank is also involved in conservation, particularly through its urban development programme, which focuses on historic city centres. Among regional development banks, the Inter-American Development Bank (IDB) has made a loan of about $29 million to Peru for a project to develop tourism in the Cuzco/ Puno area. The original budget amounted to a total of $72 million, of which about $12 million was for the conservation and preservation of monuments and sites dating from the Inca and Spanish Colonial periods.

## World Heritage Fund

One of the distinguishing features of the World Heritage Convention was the establishment of the World Heritage Fund. The fund is based upon annual contributions amounting to 1 percent of the contributions made by the member states, parties to the convention, to Unesco. The first grants made from the World Heritage Fund in 1977 were used primarily to aid member states that lacked the personnel required to prepare the documentation needed to submit natural or cultural monuments for placement on the World Heritage List (for example, the area of a natural reserve to maintain a self-sustaining ecology; or the plans, drawings, and other data for a cultural or historic monument). Since then, however, grants have also been made to train personnel, furnish equipment, and provide consultants to assist states in maintaining cultural or natural property on the World Heritage List.

## The Challenge of a New Campaign

Thus far the project that has gained the most publicity and worldwide support for conservation has been the International Campaign for the Safeguard of the Monuments of Nubia, in particular for the preservation of Abu Simbel and Philae in Egypt. Other campaigns, such as the one for Venice or for Borobudur, have been successful as well, benefitting from the stimulus of international backing and the support of Unesco. Most of the expense has been born locally; even in such cases, however, these "national" projects would not have been carried out without the catalytic role of international interest. In most cases the publicity given as part of the campaign would have been costly if carried out commercially, and the long-term benefits, such as cultural tourism, will help in amortizing the costs.

In May 1983 a new campaign was launched to help the government of Turkey preserve some of the most important monuments in

Instanbul and those found in the Göreme Valley of Cappadocia. Potentially these sites and monuments are of as much interest as those of Nubia. One has but to recall the history of Constantinople (before it was renamed Instanbul by the Turkish Republic in 1923) when it served as the capital of the Eastern Roman, the Byzantine, and the Ottoman empires. Its great ramparts preserved the city through many sieges in its long history. Emperors and sultans erected vast monuments such as the Hagia Sophia or the Suleimaniye. The city's wealth was a byword through the ages, and even today the treasures of Topkapi Palace awe thousands of visitors.

It is impossible to conceive of modern world history without taking the role of Constantinople and the Byzantine Empire into account. Europe, shattered by the fall of Rome, lived through its "Dark Ages" and the mediaeval period that followed partly because it was sheltered by Constantinople from the empires of the east. It was not until the fifteenth century that the city, a shadow of its former power and wealth, finally fell to the Ottomans. Meanwhile, in Cappadocia, monasteries were built in the soft tuff peaks, or "fairy chimneys," of a tortured landscape sculpted by wind and rain. Mural paintings record a faith that has since disappeared, but the blend of natural beauty and the work of man is being preserved and restored.

The total cost involved is conservatively estimated at $109 million, of which the Turkish government has already budgeted $31 million to initiate both projects. The campaign's goal is to raise as much as possible of the balance required. In some cases elements in the programme are similar to the Venice project in which private committees have taken over a historic building or work of art. In the case of monumental works, contributions to a general fund are required. The world economy, however, is not as buoyant as it was in the 1960s and early 1970s. The interest in international cooperation may be less apparent today than it was a few years ago. Yet these monuments represent a period of world history that should be remembered, and their preservation surely deserves worldwide support. This is one of the most intriguing challenges to be met in the current programme of Unesco.

*Bibliography*

Daifuku, Hiroshi. "Report on the International Campaign to Safeguard Historic Monuments in Istanbul and Göreme (Cappadocia), Turkey." In press.

International Committee on Monuments and Sites. "International Charter for the Conservation and Restoration of Monuments and Sites" (The Venice Charter). Paris, 1966

Unesco. *Preserving and Restoring Monuments and Historic Buildings.* Museums and Monuments Series, 14, 1972; *Venice Restored,* 1978.

———. "Victory in Nubia" (February/March 1980); "Borobudur—Rescued" (February 1983). *Unesco Courier.*

# Financing the Adaptive Reuse of Culturally Significant Areas

ISMAIL SERAGELDIN

This paper focuses on the problems of the design, preparation, financing, and implementation of a particular type of project dealing with the preservation of our cultural heritage; specifically, projects aimed at area conservation of old city centres that are being engulfed by the rising tide of urbanization.[1] Most of these cities are today in the Less Developed Countries (LDCs), where the massive scale of the challenge is matched by the paucity of resources. The World Bank has had experience dealing with these problems, notably by financing projects in Lahore (Pakistan) and Tunis (Tunisia), and a number of other projects are currently under study. These old city centres are jewels of architectural and urban design and are frequently listed as part not only of the national heritage but of the world heritage as well. Such cities as Fes, Kairawan, and Cairo have enormous treasures of buildings and urban complexes that deserve to be safeguarded.

Two key problems face conservation planners and decisionmakers. First, the present constellation of users and the uses to which the land and buildings are put are inappropriate and need change, while clearance programmes are considered politically or culturally undesirable. Second, there is a general fear that attacking the problems of restoration and conservation will be enormously expensive and that adequate financing cannot be obtained.

Our concern here is to address these two issues: first by identifying the nature of the problem; second by defining "Adaptive Reuse" as a suitable approach to the problem; and third by exploring some approaches to financing that should enable municipalities and townships to undertake such projects with minimal drain on their resources. Indeed it is probable that a well-designed project would help rejuvenate the economic base of the old part of the city and hence of the city itself. The paper concludes with the presentation of a case study, the award-winning Hafsia revitalization project in Tunis. The present phase of this project is partly being financed by the World Bank.

Darb Qirmiz quarter,
Cairo. This project,
which won an Aga Khan
Award, involved the
restoration of a group of
buildings in an old Cairo
community.

## The Special Case of Old Cities

*The Type of City*

Of specific concern here is one particular group of LDC cities: those
that have rapidly expanded around an old, traditional core, developing
a sprawling "modern" fabric around a dense "traditional" urban fibre.

Examples of such cities include Casablanca, Fes, Tunis, Cairo, and
Damascus. These old metropolises have grown by an accretion of the
"new" onto the "old," more or less concentrically, with extraordinary
expansion taking place in the last thirty years or so. The whole urban
fabric tends to exhibit a dichotomy between the new—represented by
wide roads, geometric layouts, high buildings, "high tech" irruptions,
industry, mobility, cars, and wealth—and the old—represented by
tiny patterns of streets and pathways, convoluted layouts, small
buildings, artisan workshops and small-scale industries, a more pedestrian environment, and above all, poverty.

*Defining the Problem*

*Urban Growth.* Some emerging patterns in urban growth may be noted. For example, growth at the periphery tends to leave the old city at the core (with the possible exception of Fes), and this in turn generates tremendous economic pressures for the reuse of the land in the old city. The commercial value of the land far exceeds the commercial value of the old structure on it, and the pressure to destroy old structures and replace them with new, more lucrative ones inevitably follows.

*The Human Dimension.* In spite of expectations to the contrary, the old cities retain the "spread out" population pyramids that characterize the LDCs generally. The human dimension of these demographic trends is marked by the presence of large households with many children and some older persons, all confined in a small space with inadequate areas for leisure activities and so forth. We need to know more about this human dimension—how many people are involved, what they do, what their income levels are (a particularly significant aspect), and what their social patterns are. Too many plans have focused on the buildings alone and ignored the human dimension.

*The Social Dimension.* In terms of the social dimension, we must be concerned with the ghetto-ization of the old cities. In the Maghrib countries, this has taken on a particularly clear pattern: younger generations of wealthier families have fled the old city and settled in new neighbourhoods at the periphery where modern amenities are available; their old family homes were taken over, legally or illegally, by poor tenants who subdivided the large residences to accommodate many families, thereby raising population densities and decreasing environmental quality. Gradually the old cities became receptacles for the poor and the disadvantaged—veritable ghettos. It is equally important, however, to avoid excessive gentrification—the invasion of the old neighbourhoods by wealthier "trendsetters" who buy out and displace the poor completely. This causes serious social dislocation and should be avoided, although some controlled gentrification is eminently desirable.

*The Economic Dimension.* The traditional economic base of the old city is being transformed by modernization. This is exemplified by the death of the artisan class and the entrance of wholesaling and of small machines, to say nothing of other negative incursions of modernity such as pollution, noise, and vibration. Economically, there is a drain on public funds resulting from a limited tax base with poor yields; private profits are siphoned out of the old city and reinvested elsewhere. The rejuvenation of the economic base of the old city represents the biggest single challenge to present-day planners.

*The Institutional Setting.* The first problem here is the prevalent pattern of fragmentation of land ownership, although governments and charitable religious endowments (Awkaf) own considerable tracts. Second, there is a pattern of overlapping jurisdictional responsibilities among agencies such as the municipality, the governorate, national ministries, antiquities organizations, and utility agencies supplying water, electricity, sewerage, and other services. The relative power of interested actors must be taken into account.

*The Physical Dimension.* Here we must address a number of issues: the pattern of urban form (the organic versus the grid); overcrowding; the absence of leisure facilities for the young and also the old; traffic access and parking; dilapidated and deteriorating buildings; inadequate service provision; and the challenge of protecting the rich cultural heritage of monuments of many types and ages.

*Towards a Solution*

*Some Philosophical Questions.* If we are to move towards a solution to these problems, three key philosophical questions must be addressed: (1) *What* are we trying to preserve? (key buildings? urban character? a way of life?); (2) *Why* do we want to preserve? (because these aspects are a part of our heritage? to improve the environment of the inhabitants? to earn money from tourism?); and (3) For *whom* do we preserve? (present users? future generations? the country at large? the "common heritage of mankind"?)

*Adaptive Reuse: An Approach.* Having clarified our thinking by answering these questions, we can move towards a solution to the problems of the old cities. If we concentrate first on economic and social parameters, then on physical aspects (including special consideration of conservation and preservation), I believe we can dispose of the prickly issue of renewal versus upgrading, in which we usually tend to favor upgrading based on cost aspects, displacement aspects, and cultural sensitivity. Adaptive reuse, then, is a particular type of approach, combining area preservation with upgrading, and above all a rejuvenation of the economic base of the old city.

For such an approach to work, it must focus on linkage with the rest of the city. The area in question is indeed part of the overall city, albeit a special one, and we should look carefully at economic and infrastructural links. We must also consider the need for spaces outside the perimeter if we are to reduce densities selectively by expanding shelter opportunities nearby.

Second, we should concentrate on rejuvenating the economic base. This can be done by bringing in investments and creating jobs (subject to certain nuisance factors). To do this, incentives and proper institutional mechanisms are needed within the broad framework of the tourism, services, and "high tech" options mentioned earlier.

Adaptive reuse should be accompanied by area preservation (not just single buildings), which focuses on the preservation of urban character as well as some monuments. Urban character is defined by street patterns, the proportions of buildings (not necessarily their decorative elements), the variable age of buildings on the street, and activities in the streets—a major determinant of urban character. Legislatively this means the control of new and offensive construction and the restoration and reuse of key buildings as appropriate.

A successful application of total area preservation has been made in Sidi Bou Said, Tunis. It should be noted, however, that this project involved very wealthy residents and was primarily touristic. The experience is not transferable to old cities like Cairo and Lahore.

*Rejuvenation of the Economic Base*

Given the importance of this theme in my advocacy of adaptive reuse, it is pertinent to explore the three options I mentioned earlier: tourism, services, and "high tech."

*Tourism.* The most striking vision of a marriage between economic and restoration/conservation interests is the tourism option. The ability of an attractive historic environment to draw tourists is established, and revenues from tourism should be able to finance the restoration and maintenance of historic areas. It is curious that conservationists and tourism agencies have not seen themselves as members of a natural alliance. The relationship of tourism to conservation was the subject of a conference organized by the European Travel Commission in collaboration with Europa Nostra in Copenhagen in November 1973. The conference focused on the issue of how well-managed recreational use can support and encourage conservation efforts. Convened in support of the European Architectural Heritage Year, the conference tried to encourage linkage between

tourism agencies and conservationists. Despite the many positive links
between the two parties, it seems that many conservationists are still
suspicious of the tourism option, fearing that tourism poses a threat
to the environment, both natural and man-made. While this fear may
be justified in extreme instances of commercial exploitation that
threaten to trivialize the heritage and destroy the environment, there
are sufficient examples of success and enough potential areas of
cooperation to encourage further exploration of this promising
avenue.

*Services.* A second option worth considering is the service option.
This focuses on old cities as uniquely well-placed centres for particular
types of service activities other than tourism. This option, used
selectively, could prove helpful in protecting key parts of the old
cities. An example of this approach is the work being done by the
Association pour la Sauvegarde de la Medina (ASM) in Tunis. The
restoration of thirteen old Madrassahs, at present publicly owned, is
being carried out with a view to renting the space for a viable amount
to professional associations of lawyers, medical doctors, journalists,
and architects. These groups would not only populate the Medina
but also contribute to the maintenance of the facilities once they have
been restored. This kind of creative and adaptive reuse, aimed at
matching suitable clients with the availability of space in restored
buildings, is intended to expand the economic base of the old Medina
while ensuring proper maintenance and utilization of the existing
buildings. It is one type of effort that needs to be explored further.

*High-Tech.* A third option, which is not frequently discussed but has
a great deal of promise in my judgement, is the "high tech" option.
Basically it recognizes that many new types of activities do not require
elaborate physical arrangements and can use quite small spaces.
Adequate wiring for telecommunications equipment, power supplies,
and relatively pleasant surroundings are sufficient for a wide range
of modern services, including computer-related activities and academic
think tanks. It is possible to imagine a number of high-tech firms and
service activities using old buildings and refurbishing their surroundings to match their needs and to maintain a suitable and enjoyable
environment. This would preserve the urban environment and the
architectural heritage while rejuvenating the economic base of the
old cities.

The two essential questions then are: (1) can such a project be
financed, and (2) who will pay for it? If the project is well designed

the answers should be: (1) yes, and (2) it will pay for itself. With few exceptions, good projects should pay for themselves and show a significant rate of return.

At this juncture let us pause to discuss some concepts of project finance—costs, revenues, and borrowing—and also budget management.

## Project Finance

*General Principles*

Basically there are three sources for project finance:
*Government*
  *Revenues*
  *Borrowing*
*Institutional*
  *International (and there are very few grants)*
  *Para-statal*
  *Private sector*
*Persons themselves*
  *Self-help*
  *Cooperatives*
  *Direct finance*

Ultimately if one eliminates or discounts the small grant element in international aid transfers or private charitable grants, the inescapable conclusion is that the vast majority of project costs have to be paid or repaid out of domestically generated resources; that is, from the citizens of the country.

Hence two distinct but complementary approaches are needed in dealing with public finance: (1) public sector outlays must be kept to the minimum, i.e., costs must be controlled; and (2) revenues must be increased to avoid deficit financing as much as possible.

It should be recognized that controlling costs is best done by: (1) limiting the scope of involvement, preferably generating a multiplier effect by mobilizing private resources for direct investment; and (2) limiting the standards of the proposed project to what is both affordable and feasible.

*A Public/Private Partnership*

In this instance we are focusing primarily on the renovation of old cities, which usually involves some form of redevelopment while remaining appropriately concerned with conserving and maintaining the urban character. Such developments usually have two broad components: a mixed-use development component and a residential component.

*The Mixed-Use Component.* There is no question in my mind that mixed-use projects cannot function well without a suitable public/private partnership. No private developers would move into a venture of this type without public support, since there are many logistical, legal, and other types of problems that impede an effective private-sector response to the needs of rejuvenation. Conversely a government should not try to undertake such a project entirely on its own, as it is bound to put a very heavy burden on budgetary resources and cash flow. Furthermore, implementation of such projects probably requires a managerial apparatus and technical marketing ability that are seldom found in state-run bureaucracies.

Nevertheless, it is clear such ventures require public authorities to take a leading role. They must consider themselves the prime developer in responding to a perceived need and seizing a potential opportunity.

For the public authority, the objectives of intervention are twofold: (1) to revitalize an old area by creating jobs, attracting investment, and improving the quality of the physical environment; and (2) to preserve and maintain a valuable part of the national heritage. To do so the public authority should be willing to have a limited return on its investment, if not to make an outright grant. That grant can be a very small amount of total project cost, but when appropriately positioned, it can create the seed capital necessary to launch a much bigger enterprise. On the other hand, there should be a concerted effort to avoid, under any circumstances, subsidization of recurrent expenditures, as this would create a heavy burden on the municipal or state budget.

Private developers look at matters somewhat differently. While the private sector is looking for profits, they have other prerequisites. The first thing private developers look for is the degree of public commitment to make a project work. Private developers tend to have a much easier time investing in suburban or fringe areas than they do in old town developments, and all the more so in old town restoration and rehabilitation projects as opposed to straightforward "tear down and renewal" projects. Therefore the "city as entrepreneur" has a central role to play in attracting private capital and private marketing expertise to a joint public-private partnership.

The second thing private developers look for in a project of this type is the risk-sharing element. This dimension tends to be matched with an assessment of the degree of control that the private developers will have over the part of the project with which they are involved.

Third comes the financing package. Surprisingly, a large number of private developers involved in such ventures have assured me that financing comes only third. It is important that adequate financing be provided; especially when mixed-use developments (including hotels) are involved, provision for adequate working capital is essential. The financial agreements for projects of this type invariably tend to be complex, with many factors involved. In fact it is not unusual that financial packages for old town mixed-use development projects, even without restoration/conservation components, require five to six years of negotiations with many different parties before being finalized.

Fourth, no "deal" can be effective and successful without insisting on the quality and reputation of the various individuals involved. The key lesson learned from successful public-private partnerships aimed at mixed-use developments in new and old settings alike has been never to skimp on quality expertise and consultant talent. The best marketing analysis, the best architectural design, the best construction management, and the best property management specialists are also likely to generate the easiest funding, the lowest risk, the most sensible division of management responsibilities, and an end-result well worth the effort.

*The Residential Component.* On the housing side, the question that confronts us in dealing with all cities is somewhat different. The problem is the presence of usually large numbers of poor people whose displacement is culturally, politically, and socially undesirable and whose integration into the development scheme is economically and financially difficult. Striking a balance between the needs of the poor (as well as all other residents) and the needs of the investors and likely future residents or visitors becomes one of the difficult equations on which the public and private managers have to agree. Some form of cross-subsidization is essential, and it remains the only feasible way out of this seemingly intractable dilemma.

But it should be remembered that this call to avoid a pattern of "invasion-succession" of old town neighbourhoods is not simply motivated by romanticism or altruism. It makes good business sense, as will be described below.

*The Role of the Individual*

In the final analysis individuals—as owners or operators of activities, users of services, or residents—are the ones who will pay the money (in rent or purchases) that will make or break the project.

The commercial side will be handled by the interplay of market forces, and shrewd analysts and developers will not allow the mixed-use development-restoration to stray far from the economically feasible.

Residential components are another issue. A careful evaluation of what people can afford must be made to avoid exclusion of poorer residents. This evaluation is described in figure 1 of the appendix.

## The Nature of Costs

If we accept that the private sector can accomplish most if not all of the commercial development and the government is involved in financing or assisting in financing all or most infrastructure (and occasionally superstructure) and some shelter, the financing requirements cover two main areas: (1) delivery of public services; and (2) financing of shelter per se. A brief word on each is pertinent.

*Financing the Delivery of Public Services*

The combined costs of public services (water, sewerage, etc.) and social infrastructure (schools, hospitals, etc.) account for approximately 50 percent of total expenditures in a poverty-oriented shelter programme, with approximately 30 percent due to public services. Cost recovery for these public services should be actively pursued.

*Financing Shelter*

There are two key problems in financing housing for the poor: (1) the poor usually do not have secure title to the land; hence they have no security to offer lending institutions; and (2) lending institutions have no guarantees against the risk of default by potential borrowers; nor can they effectively consider foreclosure on the basic shelters of the poor since that would be politically unacceptable.

In response to these problems, the governments of LDCs have tried to set up special financing institutions channelling their (usually subsidized) loans to the poor. This, however, raises a host of problems related to the management of indirect subsidies and the rationing of credit, which tends to freeze out the poor.

*Subsidies*

Subsidies constitute a form of income transfer; as such, some subsidies *may* be desirable as an instrument of policy in certain cases, as long as the government has the means to expand and *replicate* the subsidized programme to reach the target population. The key problem, however, is that many governments have subsidized inappropriate programmes, using deficit financing and borrowing extensively, domestically and internationally, to pay for these subsidies. As a result of pursuing this short-term political palliative, they today face intolerable debt burdens and have been unable to pursue the real long-term interests of needy citizens.

The deficits occur only because of the gap between the costs incurred and the revenues generated by governments. We have already stressed the need to limit costs. The generation of revenues is equally important.

**The Generation of Revenue: Cost Recovery[2]**

The generation of urban revenues is a key issue for governments and leads us into a consideration of principles of cost recovery. Two key complementary approaches are available to governments: taxes and user charges.

*Taxes*

Several policy principles may be considered here:

*Equity*

This involves the principle that those who receive benefits should generally pay for them, and also that repayment should be geared to the ability to pay, with the rich paying proportionately more.

*Economic Efficiency*

Efficiency is involved when taxes can channel the use of resources into productive outlets, for example, by encouraging those who own land to develop it rather than to use it only for speculation.

*Administrative Feasibility*

Will the tax be easy to collect? This becomes a crucial question in LDCs where public manpower resources may be overstrained or inefficient.

*Revenue Yield*

This is a function both of the tax rate and the tax base and must be balanced against the feasibility of collection. Inflation should be taken into account as this will affect trends in future years.

*Political Acceptability*

Whether municipalities and central governments in LDCs find the political will to practice these principles may vary according to local political circumstances. Property taxes and user charges are particularly sensitive areas. We shall now examine both these items in more detail.

*Property Taxes*

Property taxes can be highly complex, depending on the basis used for valuation.

*Annual Rental Values.* There has been a movement from the use of rental to capital values for various reasons, the most important being the difficulty of determining fair rental valuation in many countries. The information required may be unreliable in an area with little or no rented property, and in a tight rental market or in the case of rent control, regular payments may be underdeclared, with "key money" and other irregular charges ignored.

*Capital-improved Site Values.* Alternative methods of calculating capital-improved site values have been put forward. The method used usually depends on the evidence available, for example: (1) Comparing actual sales of different types of property in different locations; (2) Capitalizing rental incomes (i.e., hypothesizing capital values on the basis of rent levels); or (3) Determining construction or replacement costs for the buildings and other improvements, together with the market prices of land.

*Unimproved Site Values.* Capital values are often based upon the market value of land as a vacant site, disregarding its actual improvements. But unimproved site valuation is often considered unfair by those lacking capital to develop their property, and small businesses and low-income families are likely to be forced out of the centre of cities. Also, where the rate of return on investing in property is low, the potential advantages of this system may fail to materialize.

*Dual Tax Rates.* Because of such technical and political difficulties, authorities may levy a (lower) tax on improvement values. Site development can then be encouraged and revenue potential maximized.

*Property Valuation.* Property-tax revenues simply do not expand enough in LDC cities to meet the needs of local authorities, largely because of inadequate property valuation. Several remedies are possible. Inflation must be taken into account. Where qualified personnel are lacking, it is possible to use a simple matrix with standard variations for zone, land use, construction materials, and size. Consultants and officials from the central government may also be used to overcome shortages of skilled personnel.

### User Charges

*General Considerations.* There are four reasons for pricing public sector urban goods and services: (1) User charges provide an orderly and economically efficient (i.e., fair) method of distributing a limited supply; (2) They provide an incentive to reduce wasteful uses; (3) They provide guidelines for suppliers that help them decide how much to supply; and (4) Revenues produced lighten the burden on government budgets and often lead to a more equitable method of financing the costs of public services.

For example, if the price charged for water is too high, people might use less water than the water company is able to supply. A price set too low, on the other hand, can lead to excess demand and serious financial difficulties. In setting the price for each income group, public-sector officials should attempt to strike a balance among objectives of distributive justice, cost recovery, and resource allocation.

*Water Supply.* Consumers of water, particularly large industries, should be metered. For residential water users with metered consumption, there should be a three-tiered charging system that reflects the typical cost structure of an urban utility system. This includes, first, a use-related charge equal to the average incremental cost of water production and transmission—a periodic fee that does not vary with water use—and second, a one-time development fee. Cross-subsidies can be arranged by imposing a higher periodic fee upon middle- and high-income consumers than that which is charged to low-income consumers. For the poorest areas of a city, metering may not be appropriate. Fees can be charged according to the size of the pipe connecting the lot to the distribution network, or there can be cross-subsidy by other water users, municipal taxes, or government subsidies.

*Sewerage.* The three-tiered charging system recommended for metered water consumption can also be used for conventional piped sewer systems with a metered water supply. Large industrial enterprises should be charged fees related to the costs of their pollution.

*Drainage.* Charges for drainage—based on the length of the property line along streets—are often levied jointly with other development charges for water sewerage or road construction. However, if local financial resources permit, general property-tax financing of drainage works is appropriate for poor neighbourhoods and for financing the construction of major drainage canals for the entire city.

*Electricity.* Charges for electricity should be based on the volume of use. Peak-load problems should be built into the interaction between supply and pricing. There are considerable possibilities for tariff adjustments to provide some cross-subsidies to poorer residential users while still keeping the public utility financially viable.

*Telephone Connections.* In many LDCs there is an excess demand for telephone lines, and exchanges for the existing lines are congested during peak hours of the day. Charges should therefore be higher than the incremental costs of providing service in terms of development, connection, and use.

*Solid Waste Collection and Disposal.* Most cities impose property-tax surcharges to support the costs of refuse collection, but these do not cover costs. Supplementary charges can be imposed for collecting industrial and commercial waste, while residential refuse charges are best collected jointly with water, sewerage, and electricity charges.

*Traffic Management.* Appropriate pricing of traffic access and/or parking is an important though frequently overlooked subject. An outstanding example is the "Area License Scheme" introduced by the government of Singapore in June 1975.

*Revenue Collection*

Whatever the merits of taxes, they are of no use unless the money is actually collected. One report[3] recommends attention to the following points:

*Delegation of Authority.* The day-to-day operations of tax assessment and collection should be carried out at the local level.

*Staff Development.* Revenue departments should have their own schemes of services and salary scales, including merit increases for selected officials and upgrading of positions in line with increased responsibilities. Systematic training programmes are also essential.

*Codes and Manuals.* There should be a single code of tax laws and regulations containing an authoritative, up-to-date, and manageable statement of tax rules.

*An Appeals Procedure.* There should be an administrative appellate system to expedite the settlement of tax controversies at both lower and higher judicial levels, using judges specially trained to handle tax cases.

*Equipment and Facilities.* Tax offices should be conveniently located with adequate space for the efficient conduct of operations.

## Borrowing for Urban Development

There are three points to emphasize here: the purpose and the extent of borrowing, its sources and methods, and the importance of loan conditions.

### The Purpose and Extent of Borrowing

Public sector and especially urban officials borrow money for many reasons. These include financing short-term cash deficits; long-term capital development; income earning investment; and covering annual operating deficits. All of these mechanisms present pitfalls. Covering annual operating deficits—as experience has demonstrated—is particularly dangerous.

### Sources and Methods of Borrowing

Central credit institutions that are flexible and possess expertise have strong advantages as sources of loan finance for urban authorities.

### Loan Conditions

The prevailing market rates and the interests of the lender are paramount here, especially when some governmental and international agencies seek to keep loans relatively short (ten years), allowing them to "turn over" their lending as rapidly as possible. Loans are often repaid biannually through the life of the loan, combining repayment of principal and interest in equal installments.

### Municipal Budgetary Management

Financial autonomy for cities is very desirable because it avoids going through the treasury circuit and all the concomitant uncertainties this involves. Clearly cities cannot be absolutely autonomous, but dependence on central government should be minimized.

The following scheme by David Jones, a financial adviser for urban development at the World Bank, illustrates the flows of money which should be provided for within the accounting and budget planning arrangements of a municipality as a whole.

#### Capital Programme

An authority should plan its capital programme, including forecasts of expenditure, for a period of three to five years. The expenditure estimates for the forthcoming year (the "capital budget") should be precise and detailed enough for a recurrent budget to be prepared.

#### Revenue Budget

The revenue budget should include a comprehensive and detailed statement that shows how much the local government intends to spend on its current services during the year ahead, together with probable sources of income. After allowing for central government grants and other specific revenue sources, a local government can determine the tax scales or rate levies necessary to raise the sums required to cover anticipated budget needs.

#### Cash Forecast and the System of Flows

Some authorities prepare monthly cash forecasts and project them for a twelve-month period. Such forecasts should be updated at the least on a quarterly basis. Cash forecasts should include regular, periodical, and seasonal payments and receipts. The forecasts are important and should be done carefully so as to enable the municipality to:

- *plan in advance for the temporary investment of surplus cash;*
- *plan in advance for temporary borrowing, bank overdraft, or realization of investments;*

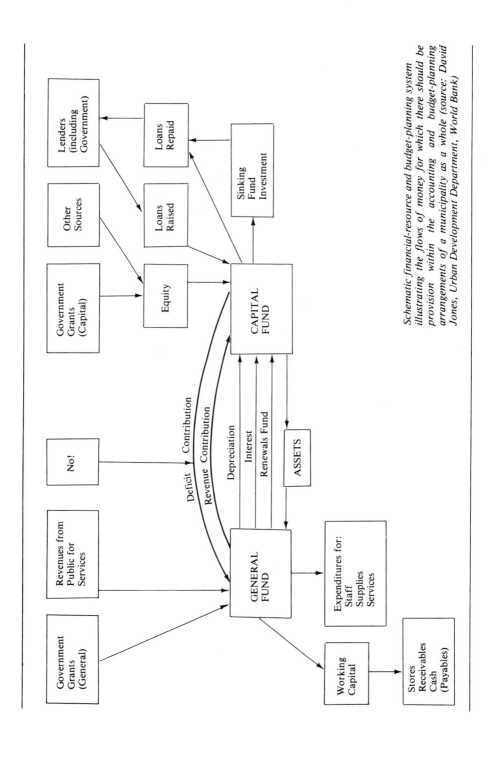

*Schematic financial-resource and budget-planning system illustrating the flows of money for which there should be provision within the accounting and budget-planning arrangements of a municipality as a whole (source: David Jones, Urban Development Department, World Bank)*

The Hafsia project was
granted an Aga Khan
Award in 1983 for its
success in solving an
urban housing problem
while retaining the scale
and ambience of the
ancient Medina.

- *plan the timing of loan-raising operations for capital works so that idle loan charges are minimized;*
- *plan the payment of creditors and bulk ordering of goods for stores;*
- *take advantage of cash discounts allowed by suppliers for prompt payment;*
- *take steps to improve procedures for the collection of income, especially at difficult periods; and*
- *minimize bank charges and interest on overdrafts.*

## An Example From Tunis: The Revitalization of Hafsia

*Introduction*

This project is an important example of applying sound economic analysis and financial discipline in the upgrading and infill part of the existing Medina. It is the second effort at dealing with Hafsia. The first effort, completed several years ago, received an Aga Khan Award for Architecture in 1983. While sensitive in concept and design, the first project was unable to cope with the needs of the poorer local residents. The present project, which is financially supported by the World Bank,[4] is designed to remedy this situation by combining sale of properties to private developers with cross-subsidization of rehabilitation loans for residential structures that have deteriorated. The present project successfully addresses the twin challenges of meeting the needs of the urban poor while showing a respectable economic rate of return on the invested funds.

**The Hafsia quarter, Tunis. New construction in an old setting.**

*Background Description*

*Location and Background.* The Medina of Tunis is the oldest area in the city. It is visibly separated from the rest of Tunis by the remains of an old city wall and by a hierarchy of roads and pedestrian paths. In 1975 the more affluent inhabitants of the Medina started moving out of their crowded surroundings into the more spacious residential developments of Tunis. They were replaced by poor immigrants from the rural areas who had moved to the capital in search of work.

Since 1954 the lower part of the Central Medina, with a total area of about 30 hectares, has been designated as a historical zone for preservation and renovation. Hafsia, with an overall area of 13.5 hectares, forms part of this lower section of the Medina. It is divided into three main sections: Sidi Younes to the west, with an area of 5.4 hectares; Sidi El Baiane to the east, with an area of 1.6 hectares; and a large central portion of 5.5 hectares of mostly vacant land.

*Existing Conditions.* Hafsia is characterized by overcrowding and by the deterioration of its buildings and infrastructure. It has a population of 4,100 inhabitants and a density of about 360 persons per hectare. Of the existing households, about 70 percent are connected to the water supply system; almost all are connected to the power supply network (about 93 percent in Sidi Younes and 97 percent in Sidi Baiane); and all are connected to an old sewerage network that is rapidly deteriorating and frequently overflows. In Hafsia, moreover,

TUNISIA
THIRD URBAN DEVELOPMENT PROJECT
Hafsia in Medina

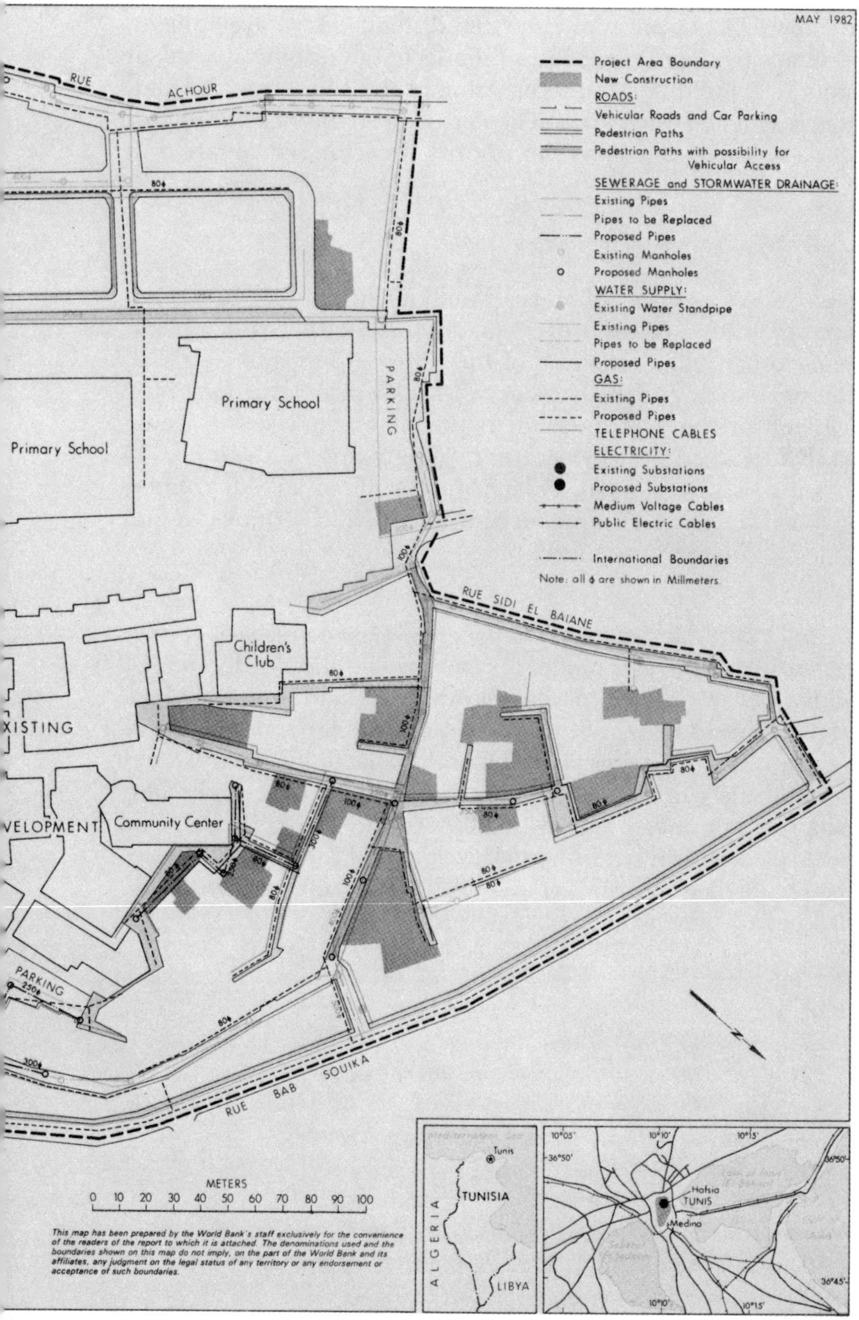

Project Area Boundary
New Construction
ROADS:
Vehicular Roads and Car Parking
Pedestrian Paths
Pedestrian Paths with possibility for
Vehicular Access
SEWERAGE and STORMWATER DRAINAGE:
Existing Pipes
Pipes to be Replaced
Proposed Pipes
Existing Manholes
o  Proposed Manholes
WATER SUPPLY:
Existing Water Standpipe
Existing Pipes
Pipes to be Replaced
Proposed Pipes
GAS:
Existing Pipes
Proposed Pipes
TELEPHONE CABLES
ELECTRICITY:
Existing Substations
Proposed Substations
Medium Voltage Cables
Public Electric Cables

International Boundaries
Note: all ø are shown in Millimeters

RUE ACHOUR

80ø

Primary School

PARKING

Primary School

RUE SIDI EL BAIANE

Children's
Club

80ø

EXISTING

100ø

80ø

80ø

DEVELOPMENT

Community Center

100ø

80ø

80ø
80ø

PARKING
250ø

80ø

300ø

RUE BAB SOUIKA

METERS
0  10  20  30  40  50  60  70  80  90  100

This map has been prepared by the World Bank's staff exclusively for the convenience
of the readers of the report to which it is attached. The denominations used and the
boundaries shown on this map do not imply, on the part of the World Bank and its
affiliates, any judgment on the legal status of any territory or any endorsement or
acceptance of such boundaries.

ALGERIA

TUNISIA

LIBYA

Tunis

10°05'    10°10'    10°15'
36°50'                36°50'

Hafsia
TUNIS
Medina

36°45'
10°10'    10°15'

there are about 2.2 hectares of empty land suitable for development. A first attempt by the municipality of Tunis to build some apartment and commercial buildings in the central portion of Hafsia in the mid-1970s was reasonably successful. The decaying conditions of the area led to the choice of Hafsia as the priority area for revitalization in the Medina.

*Project Description (See map on previous pages)*

*Upgrading.* The upgrading of Hafsia would include (1) regularization of occupancy status; (2) improvement of pedestrian roads, (3) improvement, repair, and extension of the water supply and electrical, telecommunications, and town gas networks; (4) reconstruction of the sewerage network and connection to the new trunk sewers being installed by ONAS in the city centre; (5) upgrading of about 24,000 $m^2$ of existing buildings in Sidi Baiane and 23,000 $m^2$ in Sidi Younes; and (6) construction of 90 units in Sidi Baiane and 45 units in Sidi Younes, averaging 88 $m^2$ on infill plots.

*New Construction of the Central Vacant Land.* This consists of a pilot scheme that would act as a model for the revitalization of the rest of the Medina. In view of the commercial value of land in the Medina, serviced plots would be sold to private developers for construction of the programme set out below. Simultaneously, the municipality would construct and the bank would finance Part A of Phase I of the new construction programme. Part B of Phase I and Phase II would be constructed on serviced land sold to developers. Profit from the sales would be channelled to a special account to finance upgrading. The construction in Hafsia would consist of:

> *Phase I*
>> *Part A*
>>> *(1) about 9,000 $m^2$ of new housing;*
>>> *(2) about 300 $m^2$ of new floors on top of existing shops;*
>>> *(3) about 700 $m^2$ of new shops;*
>>> *(4) about 330 $m^2$ of a secondhand clothing market;*
>> *Part B*
>>> *(1) two hotels of 1,560 $m^2$ and 730 $m^2$ respectively;*
>>> *(2) a bath house (hammam) with a area of 325 $m^2$;*
>>> *(3) an office building with about 4,000 $m^2$ of built-up area;*
>>> *(4) a child care centre of about 2,000 $m^2$;*
>>> *(5) a mosque;*

*Phase II*

> (1) about 1,000 m² of new housing;
> (2) 160 m² of new floors above shops;
> (3) three apartment buildings with an overall area of about 2,630 m²;
> (4) a third hotel of 735 m²; and
> (5) shops with an area of about 170 m².

## Costs

The cost estimates for the project are given in table 1 of the appendix. The total cost (including contingencies) is estimated to be US$18.3 million.

## Economic Impact

A careful calculation of costs and benefits for the entire Hafsia operation leads to an Internal Economic Rate of Return (IERR) of 18 percent. This estimate is robust. Even if estimates of costs are increased by 10 percent, the IERR is still a respectable 14 percent, as can be seen below:

| Assumed Case | IERR |
|---|---|
| Base case | 18% |
| 10% increase in costs | 16% |
| 10% decrease in benefits | 16% |
| 10% increase in costs and 10% decrease in benefits | 14% |
| One year delay in benefits | 15% |

## Impact on the Poor

As can be seen from the following graph, the residents of Hafsia are among the poorest in Tunis, even when compared with other poor districts of the city such as Ettadhamen and Kram Ouest. Yet careful control of costs, along with cross-subsidies and detailed analysis of what people can afford, yield an impressive result, reaching down to the twelfth percentile of income distribution in the upgrading parts. This is shown in table 2 of the appendix listing improvement charges and affordability.

## Conclusion

The skill, or genius, of the designer and the artist will come to naught if it is not supported by the hard discipline of financial realities. We need to work as much, if not more, on economic and financial policies

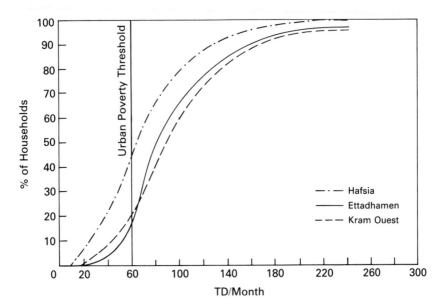

and implementation as we do on the more attractive and familiar occupations of architecture and urban design. Only the former can turn the latter from dreams into realities.

Dreams no doubt have their value. Without vision the enormous challenge of revitalizing our old cities will not be met. But that vision should be firmly grounded in the realities of today. Above all, let us not romanticize old ways of life or mystify the past. What we find quaint and attractive may be no more than a rational and economic solution to conditions that existed once but no longer exist today. It is possible, if not probable, that previous solutions will not meet the wishes and aspirations of the sons and daughters of those who formulated them, nor are they necessarily competitive in today's market conditions.

We must learn to understand what cultural continuity and the process of modernization entail; their real effects are more subtle and run much deeper than a surface comparision of building types can teach us.

Our cities, the physical expression of the social and economic organizations responsible for these processes of change, cannot remain fixed in time. Adaptive reuse of old cities is not a dilettante's luxury; it is essential for the survival of our cities as thriving dynamic centres of human activity.

## Appendix

**Figure 1**
**Making the System Affordable**

To estimate affordability of type of unit or plot, the following steps should be undertaken:

| | |
|---|---|
| *Figure* | (a) Recoverable Cost of |
| | (1) Land |
| | (2) Infrastructure (itemized) |
| | (3) Superstructure |
| | (4) Management Expenses |
| | Total Cost |
| *plus* or *minus* | (b) Cross Subsidy |
| | (1) from Market Sales |
| | (2) from Differential Pricing |
| | Total Cross Subsidy |
| *equals* | (c) Price of Plot |
| *less* | (d) Downpayment |
| *equals* | (e) Loan Amount |
| *compute* | (f) Monthly Loan Payment |
| *plus* | (g) Other Charges |
| | (1) Taxes |
| | (2) Utilities |
| | (3) Insurance |
| | Total Other Charges |
| *equals* | (h) Monthly Charges |
| *estimate* | (i) Percentage of Income Devoted to Shelter |
| *compare* | (j) Premium Monthly Income for which Unit or Plot Is Affordable |
| *define* | (k) Income-Distribution Percentile Corresponding to this Monthly Income. |

**Table 1**
**Summary Cost Estimates for Hafsia**

| | TD (000) | | | US$ (000) | | | Percent Foreign Exchange | Percent Base Cost |
|---|---|---|---|---|---|---|---|---|
| | Local | Foreign | Total | Local | Foreign | Total | | |
| A—OFFSITE INFRASTRUCTURE | **68** | **56** | **124** | **136** | **112** | **248** | 45.2 | 2.0 |
| 1. Earthworks | 2 | 2 | 4 | 4 | 4 | 8 | | |
| 2. Roads | 15 | 12 | 27 | 30 | 24 | 54 | | |
| 3. Water Supply | 1 | — | 1 | 2 | — | 2 | | |
| 4. Sewerage/Drainage | 4 | 3 | 7 | 8 | 6 | 14 | | |
| 5. Electricity | 14 | 11 | 25 | 28 | 22 | 50 | | |
| 6. Telephones | 30 | 26 | 56 | 60 | 52 | 112 | | |
| 7. Gas | 2 | 2 | 4 | 4 | 4 | 8 | | |
| B—UPGRADING | **295** | **241** | **536** | **590** | **482** | **1,072** | 45.0 | 8.7 |
| 1. Earthworks | 37 | 30 | 67 | 74 | 60 | 134 | | |
| 2. Roads | 70 | 57 | 127 | 140 | 114 | 254 | | |
| 3. Water Supply | 41 | 33 | 74 | 82 | 66 | 148 | | |
| 4. Sewerage/Drainage | 82 | 68 | 150 | 164 | 136 | 300 | | |
| 5. Electricity | 13 | 11 | 24 | 26 | 22 | 48 | | |
| 6. Street Lighting | 17 | 14 | 31 | 34 | 28 | 62 | | |
| 7. Gas | 35 | 28 | 63 | 70 | 56 | 126 | | |
| C—NEW CONSTRUCTION | **2,215** | **608** | **2,823** | **4,430** | **1,216** | **5,646** | 21.5 | 46.0 |
| 1. Land Acquisition | 393 | — | 393 | 786 | — | 786 | | |
| 2. Phase I Superstructure | 902 | 608 | 1,510 | 2,264 | 756 | 3,020 | | |
| 3. Phase II Superstructure | 920 | — | 920 | 1,380 | 460 | 1,840 | | |

| | | | | | | | |
|---|---|---|---|---|---|---|---|
| **D—UPGRADING OF SIDI BAIANE** | **840** | **588** | **1,428** | **1,680** | **1,176** | **2,856** | 41.2 | 23.2 |
| 1. Land Acquisition | 62 | — | 62 | 124 | — | 124 | | |
| 2. Indemnification | 53 | — | 53 | 106 | — | 106 | | |
| 3. Demolitions | 6 | — | 6 | 12 | — | 12 | | |
| 4. New Housing | 377 | 308 | 685 | 754 | 616 | 1,370 | | |
| 5. Addition of Floors | 57 | 47 | 104 | 114 | 94 | 208 | | |
| 6. Upgrading Existing Buildings | 285 | 233 | 518 | 570 | 466 | 1,036 | | |
| **E—UPGRADING OF SIDI YOUNES** | **707** | **529** | **1,236** | **1,414** | **1,058** | **2,472** | 42.8 | 20.1 |
| 1. Land Acquisition | 60 | — | 60 | 120 | — | 120 | | |
| 2. New Housing | 381 | 312 | 693 | 762 | 624 | 1,386 | | |
| 3. Upgrading Existing Buildings | 266 | 217 | 483 | 532 | 434 | 966 | | |
| TOTAL BASE COST | **4,125** | **2,022** | **6,147** | **8,250** | **4,044** | **12,294** | **32.9** | **100.0** |
| **F—CONTINGENCIES** | **1,991** | **1,016** | **3,007** | **3,982** | **2,032** | **6,014** | | |
| 1. Physical Contingency | 619 | 304 | 923 | 1,238 | 608 | 1,846 | | |
| 2. Price Contingency | 1,372 | 712 | 2,084 | 2,744 | 1,424 | 4,168 | | |
| TOTAL COST | **6,116** | **3,038** | **9,154** | **12,232** | **6,076** | **18,308** | | |

**Table 2**
**Hafsia Upgrading and New Construction—Improvement Charges and Affordability**

| | Upgrading of Buildings[a] | | New Buildings in Infill Plots | | | |
| | | | Option I | | Option II | |
| | Option I | Option II | Force Account or Small Firms | By Conventional Contractors | Force Account or Small Firms | By Conventional Contractors |
|---|---|---|---|---|---|---|
| Net Surface of Unit (M²) | 40 | 30 | 40 | 40 | 30 | 30 |
| Gross Surface of Unit (m²) | 50 | 37.5 | 50 | 50 | 37.5 | 37.5 |
| Cost of Land (TD/m² of gross surface) | 15 | 15 | 15 | 15 | 15 | 15 |
| Cost of Infrastructure (" ") | 3.97 | 3.97 | 3.97 | 3.97 | 3.97 | 3.97 |
| Cost of Rehabilitation (" ") | 23.23 | 23.23 | | | | |
| Cost of Construction (" ") | | | 65 | 95 | 65 | 95 |
| Total Cost/m² of gross surface | 42.20 | 42.20 | 83.97 | 113.97 | 83.97 | 113.97 |
| Connection Costs (TD) | — | — | 220 | 220 | 210 | 220 |
| Downpayment (TD)[b] | — | — | 663 | 888 | 505 | 674 |
| Loan Balance (TD) | 2,110 | 1,583 | 3,755 | 5,030 | 2,864 | 3,820 |
| Monthly Payment (TD)[c] (1st year) | 9.3 | 7.0 | 16.5 | 22.1 | 12.6 | 16.8 |
| % of Income Spent | 25 | 25 | 25 | 25 | 25 | 25 |
| Monthly Income Required (TD/hh) | 37 | 28 | 66 | 88 | 50 | 67 |
| Percentile Reached[d] | 19th | 12th | 52nd | 71st | 30th | 54th |

[a] Cost of upgrading includes land cost for municipal buildings that could be upgraded and sold.
[b] No downpayment for upgrading of buildings; 15% of total cost for new buildings.
[c] Over 25 years at 7% gradually increasing by 5% annually.
[d] Hafsia income distribution, 1981.

*Notes*

*The opinions presented in this paper are those of the author and should not be attributed to the World Bank or its affiliated institutions.*

1. This paper draws heavily upon material previously presented by the author at Cambridge, Massachusetts, in 1982. See I. Serageldin, "Project Finance, Subsidization and Cost Recovery" in *Adaptive Re-Use: Integrating Traditional Areas into the Modern Urban Fabric* (Cambridge: The Aga Khan Program for Islamic Architecture at Harvard University and MIT, 1983), 92–100. No references to that paper shall be specifically mentioned in this text.

2. This discussion draws substantially on the helpful summary of this issue published in *The Urban Edge* (June/July 1982).

3. IMF Institute, "General Aspects of Tax Administrations," Washington, D.C., November 9, 1981.

4. The cost figures and other data presented here are taken from the World Bank's appraisal report for the Third Urban Development Project in Tunisia, prepared in 1982. Although the actual figures may be slightly different, they will not significantly affect the analysis given here.

# Harnessing Science and Technology

*Realities and Paradoxes*

# Science and Technology in Architectural Conservation
## *Examples from Nepal and Bangladesh*

JOHN SANDAY

Why preserve the past? This is a question I have been asking myself ever since I became involved twelve years ago, with Unesco's safeguard programme in Nepal and, later, throughout Asia. My answers have changed from those of a young romantic, faced with the enormous challenge of embarking on a major renovation project—the old Royal Palace in the centre of the old city of Kathmandu—to those of a more seasoned practitioner, grappling with the highly contentious issues of environmental protection and the relationship of tourism to the heritage movement.

Before retracing my Asian activities with Unesco during the last decade or so, I should perhaps give a clearer picture of the somewhat unique terms of reference that Unesco and I have developed for my work. First, my activities have been predominantly in the field. There is therefore a very marked contrast between the type of work that Bernard Feilden describes in his paper and the type of work we have been undertaking in Asia. When I first arrived in Nepal in 1972, phrases such as "building conservation and environmental control" were almost unheard of. Right from the start, therefore, Unesco embarked on an extremely ambitious project that combined conservation at a highly sophisticated level with basic training and upgrading of traditional crafts skills.

### Hanuman Dhoka

The programme for the conservation of the cultural heritage of the Kathmandu Valley began as a repair and conservation programme for one of the major historic sites in the valley. This was the Hanuman Dhoka Royal Palace, or to be more precise, the Vilas Mandir, one of the largest of fourteen courtyards, or *chowks*, that make up the palace compound, set in the middle of the old city core of Kathmandu. This particular project was the outcome of a series of identification missions. These ranged from academic studies on cultural tourism to "cris de coeur" from all quarters calling for the safeguard of the mediaeval quaintness of these towns and cities of the Kathmandu valley. Action replaced words when the Hanuman Dhoka Conservation Project was launched on May 1, 1983. This was the beginning of a process that neither the Nepalese government, Unesco, nor indeed the project office itself could have envisaged beforehand. My assignment at that time was to set up a small programme of building conservation and repair—not too much in the public eye, not too contentious—as an experiment for the future. We were simply to restore a building for no other reason than its aesthetic qualities and a desire to please.

This was perhaps the first time I had to ask myself "Why preserve the past?" My first rather naive answer was—as I watched pieces of carving being cut up for firewood—to set an example to those who live in this unique environment. I no doubt felt strongly influenced by William Morris, the champion of the conservation movement in England at the end of the nineteenth century, who answered the question succinctly in the following words: "The greatest side of Art is the Art of daily life which historical buildings represent . . . What romance means is the capacity for a true conception of History for making the past part of the present."

Our project developed rapidly, and soon there was a large work force of over 200 people. Slowly we were developing special conservation techniques appropriate to the materials and structure we were working on, and it became possible at last to define the direction and purpose of the programme that was beginning to emerge. We were moving gradually towards the establishment of a training programme for administrative staff and for the craftspersons themselves. The Hanuman Dhoka Conservation Project Office had been established and recognised by the Department of Archaeology. My counterpart, Mr. Hari Ratna, had been promoted to a new post as chief conservation officer and we had already started to develop office procedures for handling what in Nepal was a sizable conservation programme, with a growing staff of draftsmen, supervisors, and conservation laboratory technicians. Each year we would take in a team of draftsmen from the local engineering institute to train them in the art of measured drawings. A training programme for tradesmen, bricklayers, carpenters, and carvers had also been established by the International Labour Office, and we were able to take on these trained people and extend their knowledge and capabilities in the field of building conservation

The author with his team of local craftspersons at the Kirtipur Tower, Hanuman Dhoka, Kathmandu, during restoration work.

and repair. The project also became a training ground for woodcarvers—a craft or guild that had almost died out. We were able to employ between thirty and fifty woodcarvers. Together with the publicity the restoration project received, this promoted a revival of the old woodcarving tradition. The subsequent tourism boom has perhaps now overcommercialized this revival.

The restored Hanuman Dhoka was the backdrop to the coronation of His Majesty King Birendra, the reigning monarch, in February 1975. This project had become the exemplar for conservation in the Kathmandu Valley, if not in all Nepal. It was at about this time that I reiterated the question, "Why preserve the past?" What benefits could be reaped from the Hanuman Dhoka Conservation Project? What, if any, would be the economic or physical returns from the investment of time and money? It was no longer possible to hide behind an academic barrier. Funds needed to finance the operation were not easy to come by. However, with the advent of tourism the pressures of western influence started to grow, and very soon the skyline around the Hanuman Dhoka, throughout the city core of old Kathmandu, was dotted with high-rise structures. The heritage of the West had arrived to modulate the fragile traditional environment of the Kathmandu Valley.

## The Master Plan

The evidence was there for all to see. It was essential now for some kind of environmental control and protection if these historic city cores were to survive.

So it was that in 1975, shortly after the coronation, and as a direct result of the success of the Hanuman Dhoka Conservation Project, Unesco was asked by the Nepalese government to field a multidisciplinary team to study the cultural heritage of the Kathmandu Valley and make general recommendations for environmental protection. After a long search and much deliberation, the team also attempted to answer our question. Their report was the Master Plan for the Conservation of the Cultural Heritage in the Kathmandu Valley.

The interrelation between development and conservation is often a point of conjecture. Environmental protection is always reckoned to be a negative factor. The team, however, preempted such statements by stating in their report that the "conservation of the cultural heritage as we understand it must never be an impediment in the struggle for better conditions, rather it should enhance this existence by investing it with that additional dimension of cultural richness which is indispensable from a 'Good life' in the fullest sense of the word."

While the master plan was being prepared, another unique and vital publication was completed. *The Kathmandu Valley—The Preservation of Physical Environment and Cultural Heritage, a Protective Inventory* is a two-volume inventory that lists, describes, and depicts with photographs and plans all the important monuments and sites in the Kathmandu Valley and sets up a protective zone around them. This project was undertaken by the Department of Housing and Physical Planning of the government of Nepal and was funded and assisted by the United Nations Development Programme (UNDP), Unesco, and the John D. Rockefeller III Fund. There are very few countries in Asia, if not in the world, that can boast of such a fine publication.

## More Than Conservation Alone

The next important development in promoting the Kathmandu Valley was the nomination of seven of the most important monuments and sites to Unesco's World Heritage List. Nepal became a party to the World Heritage Convention in 1978 and the following year nominated the following seven sites, all of which were accepted: the three Durbar squares of Kathmandu, Patan, and Bhaktapur; the two Buddhist sites of Swayambhu and Baudhanath; Changu Narayan, one of the earliest

Hindu temple complexes in the valley; and the highly venerated religious centre of Pashupatinath. The listing of these sites has become of great significance in the valley, where over the last few years the pressures of building development have become so great. For example, in the Patan Durbar Square the southern end of the palace complex was threatened with demolition because the local government wished to construct their new offices there. How is it possible that such a proposal could be entertained, especially when the Department of Archaeology was undertaking the renovation of the northern section of the royal palace as part of the cultural heritage programme? In this instance a report was made to the Ministry of Culture and Education invoking the World Heritage Convention, and we were informed that this development has been deferred indefinitely. Similarly, in Swayambhu, the local religious group was intent upon reconstructing, in a modern idiom, an important shrine that had been removed as a result of a landslide. The Department of Archaeology was informed of this construction—a concrete frame in a very exposed location on the top of the hillock. At their request a strong note was forwarded to the ministry, which gave instructions to put a stay order on the construction work. Amicable negotiations took place afterwards and a building of traditional character resulted. Perhaps an even more important result is that the local people of Swayambhu now seek our advice, as a matter of course, on any new proposals.

The International Campaign to Safeguard the Cultural Heritage of the Kathmandu Valley is one of Unesco's many campaigns to raise funds for a major conservation project. This particular project, however, can be viewed as more than just a conservation project whose end product would be a finely conserved group of historic monuments. Were the project to be implemented fully in accordance with the master plan and the subsequent economic report, an investment of US$6.25 million would be needed to finance the complete conservation and rehabilitation of all seven sites on the World Heritage List. Many other edifices scattered through the valley, amounting to a total of about 120 structures both large and small, would be preserved and maintained. It is an interesting fact that the revenue from entrance fees to the nonreligious sites and a minimal sale of guidebooks and postcards would yield a rate of return of 14 percent—a satisfactory result even in the eyes of investors and economists. Moreover, there would also be seven remarkably fine sites or conservation areas, a group of trained administrators in the Department of Archaeology, and a team of craftspersons to maintain the sites. To support the fundraising campaign, Unesco published a catalogue similar to the successful publication *Venice Restored.* The concept was expanded and a small booklet entitled *The Kathmandu Valley-Nepalese Monuments in Need of Preservation*—rather endearingly called the "shoppping list"— was produced. It identifies all the sites and monuments included on the World Heritage List, gives a brief historical description of them, notes their present condition, and makes recommendations for their repair. A photograph is also included and a "price tag" for restoration is attached to each structure. This catalogue aims at the "adoption" of each building by private individuals or national or international organizations. Project costs range from US$5,000 to $500,000.

Although nearly seven years have passed since the preparation of the master plan, this programme is very much in its infancy. Yet what little has been achieved in relationship to what still has to be done has so far been very successful. In addition to the Hanuman Dhoka project, carried out entirely by the Archaeological Department with funds from the government and from the palace's own revolving trust fund for the last six years, there have been several other building conservation and repair activities throughout Nepal.

Before we touch upon the projects directly resulting from the cultural heritage programme, I should mention the Bhaktapur Development Project, a bilateral programme funded and administered by the Federal Republic of Germany. While its main purpose is to develop services and an infrastructure for the poorest sector of Bhaktapur, much of the programme's earlier activities were devoted to the repair and conservation of many of the historic structures in the vicinity. Many of the craftspersons from Bhaktapur who had worked with us returned home to work on conservation projects and to demonstrate our techniques.

### Offshoots

Among Unesco's projects, the emergency programme to stabilize the sacred hill of Swayambhu has been one of the more dramatic. This was one of the first programmes to be funded with emergency assistance from the World Heritage Fund. Extensive research has been carried out and recommendations for a major drainage scheme to stabilize the site have been implemented over the last four years. The programme is unusual in that it required the collaboration of three different ministries in the Nepalese government and the development of specialized technology to insert the needed drainage. A very successful survey and resurvey programme has been developed to monitor any slide movement of more than one millimetre. This survey is still carried out each month during the monsoon period, when the effects of heavy rainfall activate such movement. The outcome of the stabilization programme has been very satisfactory. It has been a useful training ground for future work on similarly threatened sites. It is also hoped that because of the publicity given to Swayambhu, it will soon become the subject of a comprehensive conservation and rehabilitation project under the control of the government.

Among other projects under the programme was the renovation of the Bramayani Temple in Panauti, funded through Unesco by the French government. This particular temple was totally dilapidated. When our team started work on it, we discovered an added hazard: the structure had no foundations. This called for the development of a new technique to float reinforced concrete pads, like large snowshoes, under the main supporting columns. The concept and design were simple enough, but the execution proved difficult, as the chief priest said that we would be threatened with dire consequences should we move the stone divinity. Public relations and psychology play an even more important role than expected if literacy and certainly the comprehension of architects' drawings are almost negligible. A solution was found, and the renovation was completed successfully at a cost of about US$25,000 in just over one year.

At the same time in Banepa, just a short distance away, a small programme was sponsored by the Belgian Nepal Friendship Association, which donated funds for the repair of two little Narayan temples, the total costs of which amounted to US$8,500.

The International Fund for Monuments in New York City has undertaken the conservation and rehabilitation of a very important temple complex at Gokarna, which lies alongside the holy Bagmati River. This project has been running for the last five years with a total investment so far of about US$55,000. Within this budget, the main temple dedicated to Shiva (Mahadev) has been successfully renovated and the remarkable carvings exposed from under a totally defacing layer of glutinous black grime. It took about eighteen months just to clean the carvings around the doors using a technique, specially developed for the project, of making an ammonia and clay poultice—a simple but appropriate technology. The second stage was a totally different undertaking. A little pavilion known as the Vishnu Paduka, where important post-funerary rites take place, was on the point of structural collapse. Because of its proximity to the river and the frequent flash floods, the building was subject to added threats. Its post and lintel construction, set on a high platform, was found to be

**Gokarna in the Kathmandu Valley before restoration.**

without proper foundations within the plinth, meaning that there was no structural integrity. In such a state, it certainly could not withstand the replacement of the traditional tiled roof and could barely support the existing tin sheet covering. The structure was carefully dismantled and a new reinforced concrete foundation inserted into the plinth. After a colourful religious ceremony in which a divine foundation was also laid, the cleaned and repaired structure was once again set onto its original plinth. Once this was done, a traditional tiled roof was laid as a step towards the unification of this beautiful complex. The third stage is now halfway to completion. It consists of the repair and rehabilitation of the priests' quarters.

Perhaps the largest programme now under way is the renovation and rehabilitation of the northern part of the Patan Royal Palace, known as the Keshab Narayan Chowk. This particular project is being funded by the Austrian government, and the first stage, costing approximately US$60,000, is now almost complete. The second stage, for which US$80,000 are available, will cover the remaining sections of the courtyard and include the rehabilitation of the museum wings— the palace was formerly the Patan Museum.

Space prevents me from dwelling on the intricacies and fascinations of repairing and consolidating all the complicated and highly decorative structures on which our teams have worked. Nevertheless, in all the jobs there are common themes—all conceived in the early stages of the Hanuman Dhoka project. First, it should be pointed out that the Nepalese government makes a cash contribution of 25 percent to match any donation that is paid into the project account. Second, each project in itself is a training programme. On each of the new projects a staff member from the Department of Archaeology has been delegated not only to administer the project, but to receive further training in the methods and techniques of building conservation. Many of these staff members are now proficient in the specialized techniques that have been developed over the last ten years. Third, the efforts of upgrading and training of craftspersons are also reaping dividends, as we are today able to send to each of these projects a skilled group of trained craftspersons, who will augment their numbers with local craftspersons. Once trained, these people will be competent to maintain the structure and fabric of their local monument. What is perhaps more important is that local communities have regained both the will to do such work and pride in their accomplishments.

One of the direct results of the UNDP/Unesco involvement in the Hanuman Dhoka project has been the publication of a *Handbook of the Principles and Techniques of Building Conservation in Nepal*. My express intention in preparing this handbook was to produce something simple and practical—something that could be used as a reference for all aspects of the survey and repair of old structures. I am pleased to say that it is serving its purpose well in Nepal and indeed throughout Asia.

Thanks to the combined efforts of the Nepalese government, UNDP, Unesco, and all the many donors who have contributed to the cause, Nepal and her conservation programme have certainly made great strides in the never-ending struggle to maintain a unique environment and cultural identity. We should not be blinkered by this small success, however; the threats that still remain greatly overshadow it.

### Bangladesh: Transforming the Image

In the eyes of the media, Bangladesh is a country of starvation and devastation. To the uninitiated, it may therefore seem unreasonable to propose the need for developing a cultural heritage programme. However, with the experience of Nepal behind us, we can substantiate the reasons. In this young country the need to establish a cultural identity is even stronger and more pressing than in Nepal. Because Bangladesh had not been able to publicize its cultural heritage, an appeal several years ago for the safeguard of Paharpur went practically

**Paharpur, Bangladesh.**

unheeded. However, rather like the Hanuman Dhoka, this site later became the stepping stone to an overall, integrated programme. At an early stage in the development of the cultural heritage programme in Bangladesh, a proposal was made for the preparation of a master plan centred around two sites of archaeological and architectural importance—the Buddist Vihara in Paharpur and the historic mosque city of Bagerhat. The intention behind the formulation of this master plan has been simple and straightforward. Since Bangladesh is not an international tourist destination, the emphasis had to be different from that in Nepal. In fact these sites *are* tourist destinations but mainly for nationals—the Bangladeshis are great travellers within their own country. The need to educate and to strengthen cultural identity was apparent, and the logical corollary was to build a programme around these two sites, combining education with recreation. There would also be the chance to develop revenue-earning projects such as small museums, exhibitions, and refreshment centres under the direct control of the site administration.

A master plan has been prepared and costed, with both long- and short-term recommendations. Within its limited budget, the Department of Archaeology is implementing some of the administrative recommendations and has already initiated the recommended acquisition of land for environmental protection around the sites. On June 13, 1985, the Director-General of Unesco launched the International

Campaign for the Safeguarding of the Historic Monuments of Paharpur and Bagerhat (Bangladesh).

The daily newspapers have already given front-page coverage to the proposals for establishing a major conservation programme under the aegis of Unesco, and there have been radio and television newscasts. The projects have become household names. The Bangladesh cultural heritage programme has a fascination equal to that of Nepal, and already it is beginning to take shape. A project office, based in Dhaka, has now been established to coordinate the two projects. A guidebook is being published with UNDP funds that will describe in detail the monuments of Bangladesh. Recently the project office assisted the Department of Archaeology in filing nominations for the two sites of Paharpur and Bagerhat to be added to the World Heritage List.

Bangladesh's historic buildings probably have to contend with the most destructive natural forces threatening any building in Asia. The Bagerhat group of monuments, selected and reviewed in the master plan, are located in the Gangetic plain among the mangrove swamps. The monuments are subject to all the problems of the monsoon as well as the eroding and damaging effects of a salt-laden atmosphere.

On the practical side, we have already initiated some experiments against the chronic effects of rising damp and salt action on the brickwork. Two experiments are being carried out in the Bagerhat group of monuments: the insertion of a transfused silicone damp-proof course to prevent moisture from rising through the brickwork by capillary attraction; and the insertion of polythene sheeting to prevent the salts from leeching out of the old walls—sometimes nine to ten inches thick—into a new brick skin.

In Paharpur we are faced with an unusual challenge. This monastic site is an enclosed courtyard occupying about twenty-two acres. The enclosure walls consist of 177 monastic cells that overlook the main courtyard and the impressive remains of the central cruciform temple. Before the site can be properly presented, it will be necessary to excavate and remove at least 60,000 cubic yards of spoil from the courtyard and surroundings. This can only be done if a method of draining the site can be found. At present, even without excavating, the site floods during the monsoon.

A hydrogeologist drainage expert and an archaeologist worked together, in an unusual multidisciplinary combination, to investigate the site. They have provided us with sufficient data to cost a proposal for the master plan. Their solution was simple but effective. By careful excavation the archaeologist established the various occupation levels. Using a levelling instrument, we were able to establish the lie of the land all around the courtyard during the monastery's last period of occupation in approximately the eleventh century. The investigations proved that the original drainage flowed towards the pond or tank on the northern side—in the opposite direction of the present flow of water. It is therefore proposed that the careful installation of drains and channels leading towards the tank will control the flooding. It will be necessary to use a set of pumps for a few weeks during the monsoon; when the pond reaches its full capacity, the water will be pumped beyond the compound. Having resolved this technical difficulty, the process of excavation, restoration, and presentation can be carefully planned and carried out as a long-term programme, using the whole site as a training ground for future archaeologists from Bangladesh and, it is hoped, from neighbouring countries as well.

Various training elements for establishing a group of skilled crafts-persons are also built into the programme. This includes a strong recommendation that skilled foremen in each of the trades be permanently attached to each of the project offices.

Once the principles of such a programme have been identified, the logistics and fundraising at once become more tangible. It is hoped that, after the appeal by the Director-General of Unesco, this programme will get the attention it deserves.


### Realities and Hopes

During my travels around Asia, I have been very conscious of the fact that many countries are now interested in developing their own programmes for repairing and conserving historic monuments. More often than not, however, these programmes never get off the ground because of the lack of trained personnel, knowledge of techniques, and, perhaps more important, a clear sense of direction. Departments of archaeology, which usually have a highly trained academic staff, are struggling to conserve buildings on a largely ad hoc basis. Long-term plans of action are rare.

Yet throughout Asia there is a real will to conserve the monuments of the past. The examples are legion; some of them are sad indeed. The Palace of Leh in Ladakh, for example, represents the building style and culture of a unique ethnic group, whose land is situated to the north of the great Himalayan range. The building is now in a state of total collapse. The royal family and the people of Leh are searching for the means to restore the palace, but they admit that

The Palace of Leh, Ladakh.

undertaking such a massive project is beyond their powers. The people of Ladakh need assistance to establish direction and develop training. The will and effort of the local people must be engaged to conserve an important element of their cultural identity.

In Pakistan Unesco was asked to prepare a preservation programme with special reference to the development of tourism. In its report, prepared in collaboration with the Department of Archaeology, a team of consultants set out an overall programme of conserving and presenting the wide variety of monuments and sites. The document has become a useful tool for the government, and already Unesco has been requested to carry out a more detailed study of a group of Hill Forts in the Karakoram. However, it is important that a programme with a broader spectrum be developed in Pakistan. Besides the development of special techniques, the training and upgrading of specialized craftspersons—such as those who work on stone inlay work or are familiar with the special technique for glazing bricks and tiles—is essential to the retention not only of the monuments but of the country's traditional identity.

Most of the programmes I have outlined here are small compared with some of the magnificent major restoration projects—for example, Philae, Borobodur, and even the Acropolis in Athens—that have been undertaken with Unesco's assistance. However, Unesco's programmes in Asia are in fact far more oriented towards the creation of necessary infrastructures within the various departments of archaeology, and towards helping them to establish training and educational programmes for administrators as well as for the specialists actually conserving monuments or sites. The final result will be the perfectly conserved historic monument that can be used as an educational setting for the general public: to teach nationals the importance of their own cultural identity within the framework of mankind; to offer foreign visitors yet further treasures of a common human heritage; and finally, to help us all answer the question "Why preserve the past?"

# Saving Indonesia's Borobudur
## A High-Tech Triumph in International Cooperation

W. BROWN MORTON III

The richly carved stone terraces of Borobudur, the largest Buddhist monument in the world, rise in orderly majesty above the tree tops of central Java. Not quite a pyramid, not quite a stupa, this twelve-hundred-year-old temple is a masterpiece of Indonesian culture and unique in world architecture. It also provides an education in what international cooperation can achieve when science is placed at the service of the cultural heritage. Borobudur is a shining symbol of the founding ideals of Unesco. In particular it exemplifies Unesco's responsibility, defined in its constitution, to "maintain, increase and diffuse knowledge by ensuring the conservation and protection of the world's inheritance of books, works of art and monuments of history and science."[1]

On February 23, 1983, people from all over the world were welcomed to Borobudur to celebrate the completion of the Borobudur restoration project. The Director-General of Unesco, Mr. Amadou-Mahtar M'Bow, commented on that occasion, "Unesco's objective has been a dual one: firstly to rescue works testifying to man's creative genius, his intuitions and hopes, and to his quest for the absolute; secondly to make these works accessible to the people at large . . . both the people whose heritage they constitute, who can rediscover in them the proof of their cultural identity and of their continuity in time, and the other peoples of the world who are beginning to regard such works as a part of a single heritage. The indivisible heritage of mankind as a whole—Borobudur is a pre-eminent example of such works."[2]

Unesco's involvement with Borobudur began in 1955 when the newly independent Republic of Indonesia requested Unesco to provide technical assistance in evaluating the historic preservation problems facing Borobudur. Over the next twenty-eight years the project grew to become one of Unesco's major international campaigns. Over U.S.

**Borobudur, Indonesia. Dismantling and reassembly of the temple in progress.** *(Photo: Unesco/A. Gunn.)*

$20 million were spent to dismantle, conserve, and reassemble over 800,000 stones and to stabilize the temple against earthquakes and torrential rains.

The origin of the word Borobudur itself is obscure. There is general agreement, however, that the monument was built sometime between 780 and 856 A.D. and formed the central feature of a Buddhist monastery complex. Borobudur is essentially a stepped dry stone pyramid built on the rise of a low hill. The structure is composed of nine stone terraces rising to a bell-shaped stupa at the top. The first six terraces are square in plan. The balustrades and walls of the square terraces are covered with 1,460 panels of exquisite bas-relief sculpture representing scenes from sacred Buddhist texts. The topmost three terraces are circular in plan. The first terrace is 403 feet square at the base and the monument rises to a height 105 feet above grade. Borobudur is built of dressed, grey-brown volcanic stone constructed around a core of earth fill. It is laid up without mortar in an intricate interlocking pattern to permit slight movement without danger of collapse in the case of seismic activity or minor settlement. Borobudur is oriented on a north-south, east-west axis, and access to

Borobudur, Indonesia. A seated Buddha from the temple. *(Photo: Unesco/D. Roger.)*

the top is provided by steep stairs leading up the center of each face. These four staircases also provide access to the nine terraces. The monument has no interior space; it is a Buddhist holy place of pilgrimage and symbolizes through its form and plan the Buddhist concept of the organization of the cosmos and the path man must take through it to achieve enlightenment.

In the ninth century, the builders of Borobudur conceived of it as a model of the three levels or "worlds" of the universe. The base of the monument represents the world of desire (*kamadhatu*), or the state of spiritual development where human beings are still the prisoners of their own desires. The five square terraces above the base represent the world of form (*rupadhatu*), where one has mastered dependence on desires but is still bound by the laws of form and matter. The three circular terraces and the final stupa represent the world of formlessness (*arupadhatu*), where a person is freed from all earthly ties. The original base of the monument, with a series of 160 bas-reliefs representing the "world of desire," was covered up at some early stage with an encasement of nearly 13,000 cubic meters of stone, probably to prevent slippage and settlement. This "hidden foot" of

Borobudur was not rediscovered until 1885. Portions of the original bas-reliefs have now been exposed to view. The square terraces of the "world of form" have narrow walkways encircling the pyramid. These walkways are flanked by high ornate stone balustrades with sculptured panels and hundreds of niches, each containing a statue of a seated Buddha. The ornate decoration of these terraces and the visual and physical confinement of the terrace walkways reinforce the symbolism of *rupadhatu* and give Borobudur its essential character when seen from a distance. At the sixth level, the visitor passes through a small cramped archway and emerges out onto the three upper levels of the monument, into the "world of formlessness." The actual experience of this transition is as dramatic as a clap of thunder. The plan of the monument changes from square to circular. The elaborate carved panels and niches cease. The upper terraces are virtually free of decoration. The high, confining balustrades vanish and one can see out freely from horizon to horizon in all directions. Arranged in quiet repose around the upper terraces are three rings of pierced stone stupas each containing a statue of a seated Buddha. The main stupa at the top of the monument is severely plain and carries no decoration at all. Borobudur is the masterpiece of Mahayana Buddhism and one of the outstanding examples of religious art in the world.

Although the early history of Candi Borobudur is not well recorded, it is probable that the monument fell into disuse sometime before the fifteenth century when the people of Java converted to Islam. Borobudur was rediscovered in 1814 during the brief period of British occupation of Java. The Lieutenant Governor-General of Java, Sir Thomas Raffles, had a report of the structure prepared by Cornelius, a Dutch engineer. The first scholarly monograph on the "Hidden Foot" of Borobudur, uncovered in 1885, sparked wide public interest, which in turn led to a decision by the Dutch colonial government to stabilize and restore damaged sections of the structure.[3]

Because Borobudur is built of cut and fitted volcanic stone blocks assembled without mortar around a central core of sandy clay, there has been movement and settlement since the very beginning of construction. A close examination of the structure has revealed constant adjustments and rectification of the stone courses as the building went up.

Over the centuries intermittent seismic activity, water penetration, the uncontrolled growth of vegetation, vandalism, and neglect had taken their toll. Walls had cracked and leaned badly out of plumb. The upper stupa and most of the small perforated stupas on the upper terraces had collapsed, and many of the statues were missing in whole or in part. The movement of the walls had caused major damage to bas-relief sculptured panels. Uncontrolled water seepage had weakened the clay fill and encouraged deterioration of the surface of both plain and sculptured stones.

A commission was appointed by the government in 1900 to prepare preservation and consolidation plans. A Dutch army engineer, Theodoor Van Erp, was put in charge of the project. Work began in 1907 and was completed in 1911. Under Van Erp the site immediately surrounding the Candi was excavated, the lower terrace wall was consolidated, and extensive repairs were made to the balustrades, stairways, arches, and niches. The major work was the virtual dismantling and reassembling of the fifth terrace balustrade, the three upper circular terraces, and the top stupa. From the time Van Erp finished his work in 1911 until the beginning of the current project, very little conservation activity other than routine maintenance took place at Borobudur.[4]

The present project began to take shape in 1955, a few years after the Republic of Indonesia became a member state of Unesco. At that time the first of a series of consultant experts from Unesco traveled to Borobudur to advise the government's Archaeological Institute. The outcome of the consultations was the decision to undertake a massive restoration and stabilization program to rectify the severe structural problems, caused by continued settlement and water damage, and to try to reduce the alarming deterioration of the sculpture and carved decoration. From 1971 to 1973, the organization of the final project took shape. The government formed the Badan Pemugaran Candi Borobudur (BPCB), the Agency for the Restoration of Candi Borobudur, and also approved a comprehensive preservation project developed by the Netherlands Engineering Consultants (NEDECO). Unesco agreed to organize an international campaign to raise funds for the project and also appointed a Unesco coordinator for monuments and sites in Indonesia to work with the staff of the BPCB. To monitor the work in progress and modify the work program if necessary, the government of Indonesia formed a Consultative Committee for the Safeguarding of Borobudur. The members appointed to the committee were Professor Roosseno, chairman of the BPCB; Dr. D. Chihara, Japan; Dr. K. Siegler, Federal Republic of Germany; Dr. R. M. Lemaire, Belgium; and Mr. J. E. N. Jensen, United States. In 1975 Mr. Jensen retired from the committee and was replaced by the author. An executive committee was also created to manage project funds.

The International Campaign for the Safeguarding of Borobudur was officially launched on December 6, 1972. Over the next decade, more than six-and-a-half million U.S. dollars were donated by twenty-eight countries[5] and eight private nongovernmental organizations.

The private nongovernmental organizations included the following: America Committee for Borobudur, Inc.; Borobudur Restoration Supporting Group in Nagoya, Japan; Commemorative Association of the Japan World Exposition; General Lottery in the Netherlands; International Business Machines Corporation; Japan Association for the Restoration of Borobudur, in cooperation with the Asian Cultural Center for Unesco; John D. Rockefeller III Fund, New York; and the Netherlands National Committee for Borobudur.[6] The major share of the cost, however, was met by the government of Indonesia.

The preliminary project report, "The Restoration of Borobudur," issued by NEDECO in 1972, identified three principal causes of deterioration: (1) dramatic acceleration in the rate of deterioration of the bas-relief sculptures, the statues, and the other surface stones caused by physiochemical and microbiological attack; (2) inadequate drainage; and (3) severe settlement cracking and subsidence, especially of the first, second, third, and fourth terrace and balustrades, caused by insufficient bearing capacity of the soil beneath the monument and uncontrolled washing away of the soil fill in the center of the monument.

The report called for a series of preservation measures to stabilize Borobudur and to reduce further deterioration to a minimum. These measures included the following: (1) installation of a drainage system to provide rapid run-off for rainwater; (2) introduction of waterproof layers to prevent further water infiltration and seepage; (3) introduction of reinforced concrete slabs under areas of heavy compressive load to distribute it evenly over a wider area; and (4) cleaning, consolidation, and repair of bas-relief panels, statues, and other stone decoration.

It was decided that the preservation work would include the four square terraces and their balustrades, and the plateaus between the fourth square terrace and the first circular terrace, but it would not include major work to the ground-level encasement surrounding the hidden foot or work on the three circular upper terraces and the final stupa. The work done by Van Erp on these areas had held up adequately.

Extensive research was undertaken prior to the adoption of the final project design. A multidisciplinary scientific approach was adopted, involving an impressive array of skills including aerial photo analysis, archaeology, architecture, chemistry, conservation, engineering, seismology, foundation engineering technology, landscape planning, meteorology, microbiology, petrography, physics, soil mechanics, surveying, and terrestrial photogrammetry.[7] The Borobudur project was definitely "high tech."

The execution of the work required the removal, treatment, and replacement of all of the outer stones and many of the inner stones of the affected areas. Over 800,000 stones were moved in the course of the work. In addition to the reinforced concrete slabs installed to distribute the compressive loads evenly, the scheme called for the installation of a sophisticated series of waterproof layers. One layer of Araldite-tar-epoxy was painted over the surface of reset inner stones to prevent seepage between the filled earth core of the monument and the outer stones; a vertical layer of treated inner stones was covered with Araldite-tar-epoxy two courses behind the outer decorated stones to prevent moisture moving through the decorated stones by means of capillary action. There is a third layer of asphalt on the underside of the reinforced concrete slabs. There is also a system of hidden drain pipes installed flush with the concrete slabs and beneath the open joints of the relaid terrace floors to carry away rainwater runoff. A filter layer of volcanic sand to improve drainage is also provided within the wall at each terrace level.

In order to carry out and complete the work, the following breakdown of tasks was developed by NEDECO: (1) dismantling, transport, and storage of outer stones; (2) cleaning, repair, and treatment of outer stones; (3) construction of the reinforced concrete foundation slabs; (4) transport and treatment of the inner stones; (5) insertion of the filter layer and waterproof layers; and (6) replacement and reconstruction of the stones of the main walls and balustrades.

NEDECO also devised an ingenious system to transport the stones from the monument itself to the work area southwest of the hill on which the pyramid is built. The transportation system included: (1) a series of small, hand-operated cranes at all levels for transporting individual stones from their original location to specially designed wooden pallets; (2) tower cranes on tracks for vertical transport of the stones in the wooden pallets from the terraces to the ground; (3) forklift trucks for transporting pallets to the crane gantry at the southwest side of the hill; (4) a crane gantry for transporting pallets from the hilltop to the working area at the foot of the hill; and (5) forklift trucks for transporting pallets in the working area and to the temporary and final storage areas.

The dismantling of the stones was achieved by working simultaneously on opposite faces of the pyramid so as not to disturb the equilibrium of the monument. The balustrades were taken down first, then the inside terrace walls and floors, and finally the inner stones. Each outer stone was numbered, moved, inspected, cleaned, disinfected, treated, repaired, and stored for eventual replacement on the monument.

All stones were recorded by conventional photography and by stereophotogrammetry, and then an innovative computer program was devised to number and trace the path of each stone through the complicated preservation sequence.

The development of this computer program remains the single most outstanding technological achievement of the Borobudur project. The program was developed by IBM in cooperation with the government of Indonesia. A detailed report, "Computerized Stone Registration System for the Restoration of Candi Borobudur," by V. K. Khandelwal and M. Soepardi, was published by the Badan Pemugaran Candi Borobudur in 1977.

Some of the problems to be solved by computer were: (1) numbering and recording of over 400,000 outer stones; (2) numbering of pallets; (3) keeping track of each stone as it moved through the preservation process (not all stones required the same treatment in the same order, but all stones required some treatment); (4) organizing temporary storage space before treatment and final storage after treatment but before rebuilding (this was complicated by the fact that dismantling was carried out from the top down and rebuilding carried out from the bottom up; also dismantling areas on the monument were not in the same sequence as rebuilding areas); and (5) the number of wooden pallets was limited and had to be efficiently used.

The major benefits of the computer program for Borobudur were: (1) ensuring the proper and timely treatment of stones; (2) analysing the efficiency of the overall project operation; (3) ensuring proper coordination between different project phases and identifying and correcting delays; (4) planning for rebuilding when sufficient stones were ready; (5) providing adequate project documentation; and (6) checking errors, duplication, and losses.

The development of the computer program for Borobudur has revolutionized large-scale preservation project planning and will clearly have a significant impact throughout the world when projects of a similar complexity are undertaken.

The great success of the project has been largely due to two principal factors: the flexibility of the organizational structure of the project design, which permitted Indonesian, bilateral, and international participation in a coordinated manner; and the unflinching commitment to technological, multidisciplinary research and the application of that research to develop integrated solutions to the complex conservation problems Borobudur presented.

The January 1983 *National Geographic Magazine* article, "Indonesia Rescues Ancient Borobudur"[8] refers to the Borobudur project as a "triumph of historic preservation through international cooperation." It is hoped that present and future generations will agree.

*Notes*

1. Unesco Constitution.

2. Amadou-Mahtar M'Bow (Address given at the ceremony to mark the completion of the International Campaign to Safeguard Borobudur, February 23, 1983).

3. W. Brown Morton III, "The Preservation of Borobudur, Indonesia," *Parks Magazine* 2, No. 4 (January–March 1978).

4. *Proceedings of the International Symposium on Candi Borobudur.* (Tokyo: Kyodo News Enterprise, 1981).

5. The twenty-eight countries are: Australia, Belgium, Burma, Cyprus, Federal Republic of Germany, France, Ghana, India, Iran, Iraq, Italy, Japan, Kuwait, Luxembourg, Malaysia, Mauritius, Netherlands, New Zealand, Nigeria, Pakistan, Philippines, Qatar, Singapore, Spain, Switzerland, Tanzania, Thailand, United Kingdom.

6. Soekmono, *The Restoration of Candi Borobudur at a Glance.* (Jakarta: Ministry of Education and Culture, February 1983).

7. *Report of the Executive Committee to Safeguard the Temple of Borobudur,* 11th Session, Yogjakarta, February 21 and 22, 1983.

8. W. Brown Morton III, "Indonesia Rescues Ancient Borobudur," *National Geographic Magazine* 163, No. 1 (January 1983).

# Science and Technology in Architectural Restoration
## An American Perspective

MAXIMILIAN L. FERRO

The preservation of our cultural environment can and should be seen as a timeless and endless task, carried out more through traditional skills and inherited craftsmanship than through technological virtuosity. Cyclopean walls built through Herculean effort are often maintained by patient perseverance.

Unfortunately, mankind's natural reverence for the achievements of past generations is sometimes subject to cataclysmic lapses, during which the work of centuries may fall prey to war, religious intolerance, or ideological contempt.

While 1945 found Europe and other regions burdened with the rubble of the last great global conflict and the United States virtually unscathed, it was in this country that the cultural environment was to suffer its greatest postwar abuse. Mesmerized by the vision of shiny new cities and by the lure of plentiful and inexpensive energy left disposable by the cessation of hostilities, the United States destroyed its cities while many countries of the world were rebuilding theirs.

In industrially developed countries such as ours, marrying science to conservation is not a problem of understanding specific scientific techniques (which are available for the asking) but one of the cultural climate within which these techniques may or may not be constructively applied. I believe that in the United States we are witnessing the first great change in cultural climate since World War II.

In 1776 when the country was born, America was very similar to many of the "underdeveloped" or less-developed countries in the world today in that the entire cultural environment was made of handcrafted material. The buildings in which people lived, the utensils they used, and the furniture that surrounded them were entirely the product of craftsmanship. Artisans held very important positions in early America; they were respected as an especially important part of American culture.

The Industrial Revolution is often credited with the demise of craftsmanship. I would suggest that this is not the case. In fact, at its first centennial in 1876, the United States was a country that stood at the very apex of its early industrial revolution. But that time was also a high point of genuine involvement on the part of the artisan, which existed in America (and *still* exists in so many countries) only a few decades ago.

The automobile is often blamed for the demise of the craft ethos. Indeed the automobile brought a whole new architecture to this country—what we now lovingly refer to as "bungaloid." It brought the rise of the American suburb. It enabled people to live much further away from their work place than was ever thought possible before. But interestingly enough, the architecture of early suburbia in the United States was *not* a poorly crafted architecture. On the contrary it was an architecture of consummate quality. I have a large collection of homeowners' catalogues from the 1920s, and when we thumb through these catalogues, we find the finest of materials. People were proud of their new independence, of owning a single-family home for the first time, and as a result they looked to clay tiles and slate, to metal roofing, to copper flashing—all of the things that are now considered the highest order of craftsmanship in construction. Radiation was invariably cast iron, and continued to be—this being the finest material for the purpose—until cast iron became a strategic material in World War II and the bad drove out the good.

The Depression was the stultifying experience that destroyed craftsmanship and the craft ethos in the United States. Alas we arose from the Depression on the wings of war, creating a great postwar boom. This was fueled by the fact that energy was less expensive in 1945 than it was when we had prepared to fight the great war that had now come to an end. And because of that, and because of the need to put hundreds of thousands of returning servicemen back to work, we created a construction industry in this country that was based on relatively high wages to give these people an opportunity for what we then called the American dream. The incredibly low energy costs enabled us to use materials *wastefully*.

The result was, I suppose, the American dream—the fight to have a picture window that looked into the picture window of your neighbor across the street. We destroyed the past; we destroyed it shamelessly. When I was going to school, we spoke of "kleenex architecture." We said that any architect that built a building that would last longer than twenty years was *robbing* his client. He was a fool because once the building was amortized, there was no more reason for that building to exist and it merely stood in the way of progress.

What few buildings were saved, were preserved for romantic purposes. There were many great monuments of folly among them. In Houston, Texas, for example, only seven buildings from the past have been preserved, and they are preserved in the middle of skyscrapers in a cute little thing done by the ladies auxiliaries and the Junior League called "Sam Houston Park." If you suddenly feel the need, you may go and pat an old building and move on.

The rest of the old buildings in the United States were either torn down or simply left to fall down. We lost all interest and all empathy with our own cultural roots. Buildings were bulldozed by the thousands to make room for roads to take us ever elsewhere. The average American in the postwar period only stayed in his home for four years. He did not grow to love that home; he merely viewed it as a passing stage in his economic development. If repairs had to be made, they were done with expediency. Why waste money on something that you are about to divest yourself of?

There was always someone ready to buy that home. He or she was called an "emptor" and was supposed to "caveat" but usually didn't, fortunately, so that you could always sell the house no matter how ill maintained. Materials in our hardware stores became of incredibly low quality. To a certain degree this is still true today. It is just beginning to change. It is *not* at the local hardware store that you will find the interaction between science and conservation of buildings.

I took some of my graduate students to a hardware store. Of course the great myth in the United States today is that all of our wooden buildings, which represent the majority of vernacular buildings in this country, are doomed because "you can't paint buildings any more." To a large extent, whether you can paint the building or not depends on whether you can first caulk it properly to prevent infiltration of moisture underneath the paint layer. I asked the hardware store owner for his finest caulk, and he gave me the best caulking he had, a tube that costs seventy-nine cents and is slightly less effective as a caulk than Colgate toothpaste. In the marine section of the hardware store, he did have, by coincidence, the very caulking that I usually specify for paintable wood-to-wood applications: Boatlife Lifecaulk, a paintable polysulfide that meets all government specifications. The first caulking does not meet anyone's specifications, expect possibly those of the company that makes it. The proper caulking compound costs ten times as much as the first—US$7.95 a tube. The difference is that it is a caulking compound. It does the job. You will not have to repaint your building after a year and a half.

Gradually hardware stores began to stock overwhelming supplies of low-cost, ineffective materials: caulk that did not seal, putties that dried out, woodfillers that shrank, paint that peeled, and countless other products designed only to correspond to short-term goals. Those of us who had an abiding interest in long-term building conservation were inexorably pushed out of the mainstream of American construction.

Thus by the dawn of the 1970s, conservators responsible for the maintenance and restoration of national monuments or other irreplaceable historic structures could find little solace on store shelves and increasingly opted for epoxy consolidants, woodfillers, lead paints, and other materials they could mix in their own laboratories. Like art conservators before them, architectural conservators turned to chemistry and the applied sciences for their special needs and, in so doing, began to compare notes and frustrations. The Association for Preservation Technology (APT), jointly founded by Canadians and Americans in 1968, was an attempt to compare such notes internationally; its first technical bulletin was published in 1969 with the help of the Canadian National Commission for Unesco.

Unfortunately, our construction industry has evolved in such a way that the man who chooses the caulking is the painter who has just been awarded the whole painting job on a low-price bid. Your chances, therefore, of having anything remotely like a caulking compound used on the building are nil if you happen to be simply a homeowner repainting a house. Of course if you are an architect, you tend to think you will specify the right thing, but in this country the architect, knowing that the warranty lasts only one year, has traditionally traded off the difference between the true caulking and some useless substance for some item that is forgotten elsewhere in the contract.

In America the warranty period became a single year after World War II. This essentially means that it was totally dictated by the industry. It also means that by the time you find out there is a problem with the building, it is too late. No one is liable except the unfortunate person who owns it. In Quebec, however, where I was educated under the Napoleonic Code, the warranty is ten years. And after those ten years, if the owner of a building feels that he has just cause to believe that something is not yet worn-out but shows *signs* of failure, he may automatically petition the court for a full ten-year extension over the entire building, making that warranty in effect a twenty-year one.

Buildings are not significantly more expensive in the province of Quebec, but they have always been built more carefully.

All this began to change a few years ago with the awareness that we would have to pay Third World countries for their national resources. What the rise in energy costs did to this country was to cause a sudden, sharp, and inexorable rise in the cost of building materials. In 1974 I built myself a house with several thousand bricks—the finest bricks that money could buy—and I paid seven-and-a-half cents a brick. In 1980 I built myself a patio with the selfsame bricks and paid sixty-six cents a brick. In that period prices increased as sharply as 45 percent per annum for certain classes of materials—at a time when we were suffering inflation in the range of 15 to 18 percent, and at a time when the cost of labor was increasing at an annual rate of 12 percent.

The government gave us the great equation that in order to make bricks—to mold them and to fire them—you must expend the energy equivalent of one gallon of gasoline for every eight of those bricks. That is why a brick could go in a few short years from seven-and-a-half cents to over sixty.

New construction continues to be material intensive. It takes a long time to teach builders a new way. It took decades to evolve the kind of construction that we have now, and it is going to take decades to improve it. Rehabilitation, on the other hand, is labor intensive. Indeed work has to be done. There is an economy of materials due to the fact that the materials are already there. Thus while preservationists like myself would love to take credit for having brought about a change in America—from new construction and the despoilment of our heritage to a tremendous new wave of rehabilitation—that credit belongs to the old concept of "the bottom line."

The effect of rising energy costs in America has been to demonstrate the long-term advantage of rehabilitation over new construction. And since I am one of those people who does not believe we will solve all our problems through solar energy in the next two or three years, this is going to remain the most important point in the construction industry in the United States for decades to come.

In Massachusetts, between 1974 and 1976, we saw a change in the total construction dollar—from 70 percent new to 30 percent rehabilitation to the opposite, 30 percent new to 70 percent rehabilitation. The American Institute of Architects predicts that over 80 percent of all construction dollars spent in this country by the end of the 1980s will be spent on existing buildings. Yet we have 103 architectural schools that are teaching absolutely nothing about rehabilitation.

The new economic climate in this country dictates "keeping what we already have." Some of it has been very glamorous. Quincy Market in Boston is the only place in America that now attracts more people than Disneyworld. But the real lesson is not in the glamorous projects but in what I would call "vernacular conservation." I have coined a phrase that I am using more and more with my students—the philosophy of minimalism. We are returning to concepts like permanence, beauty, and economy; we can begin to use the words together again. We are now talking about cost effectiveness; we are talking about life-cycle costing.

Take, for example, the beautiful school—built by a wealthy man, who gave it to his hometown in 1904—that our firm recently restored. Everything was done the best way known in 1904. The man even left a generous fund for the building's maintenance. The city thanked him by appropriating the funds for city expenses and not spending a single penny on this building from 1904 to 1980. Fortunately the town next door had an equally beautiful school and they chose to tear it down. They spent $22 million building a school that will last at most twenty-five years. At this point the first town realized that it would like to keep its school a little longer, and we were able to study the building and start the long process of determining what aging had taken place.

Conservation really begins with the laborious observation of how the building has aged. This means looking at the erosion of mortar and the micropitting of copper, and then bringing back the traditional crafts, which have been dormant in the United States but are still known. These crafts are necessary to reverse the aging process.

The wonderful thing about the new emphasis on conservation is that it is putting the United States back to work to a degree that was not even thought possible five years ago. Moreover, our workers never liked being dehumanized. After World War II it did not matter whether a bricklayer knew how to lay an intricate brick pattern or a beautiful straight wall. The only thing that mattered was how many bricks were laid per hour. Under those rules, even the finest craftsperson in the world can become a robot. And we *have* turned our craftspersons into robots. It is surprising how the atmosphere of ill will and the general irritability typical on new-building construction sites disappear when workers are engaged on a rehabilitation project.

Building the same school in concrete today would have cost between $70 and $90 per square foot. It would have cost $14 to $20 million to build a high-quality building in the modern idiom, and $25 to $30 million to build a replica of the eighty-year-old building. That same building was totally rehabilitated. The outside envelope was made absolutely new again for $825,000, using all the finest materials. New heating brought us up to the enormous figure of $13.07 per square foot. The low cost was due to the building's inherent *quality.*

It is because of equations like this that we can now turn to an organization like the Association for Preservation Technology (APT), born out of the joint efforts of both Americans and Canadians. The organization at first spoke to very few people and concerned itself only with those few buildings and sites in America that we had somehow allowed to stand—Mount Vernon and a few select others. Yet it made it possible for North Americans engaged in long-term cultural restoration of the built environment to proudly pursue their still unfashionable interests within the supportive climate of their own professional organization.

Although we had the technology, we did not have the public's attention until five or six years ago. The fifteen years since the birth of APT have seen some extremely rapid changes. Many were sparked by the rise in energy costs, which, by sharply increasing the prices of new building materials, quickly buried the vision of the ever-changing, regenerating city. By the late 1970s, the mounting cost of materials had shifted the balance from material-intensive new construction to labor-intensive rehabilitation, and tax incentives recognizing the advantages of such a shift were put into place in 1976 and 1981. Since the early 1980s, the once seldom-practiced art of rehabilitation has expanded to include at least 75 percent of the total building industry, with even higher statistics now routinely quoted for the later years of the present decade.

Now we have the public's attention. As cultural restoration is transformed from an elitist pursuit to a full-fledged mass movement, the preservation scientists and technologists who have formed the backbone of APT must learn to assume an unfamiliar and far more public role. Specifically, leadership is urgently needed in the creation of equitable but realistic technical rehabilitation standards, which could bring to renovation the same clarity of recognized performance levels already enjoyed by new construction. Just as we can express the quality of lumber with universally recognized precision we must become able to express the efficacy of a consolidation process.

APT has joined forces with the American Society for Testing and Materials (ASTM) in this urgent and historic task. This will necessitate a broadening of APT membership, particularly with the inclusion of industry and producers, so the association will be more truly representative of the society it serves.

We are already on our way, I think, to a new age of American craftsmanship and a new concern for our past. As I said at the beginning, in a fully developed nation it is not all that difficult to tackle the technical problems. This is a pivotal year with respect to the influence of science and technology on cultural restoration. With sharply mounting interest in effective rehabilitation, we will have a very receptive market place and an attentive public. No greater opportunity has presented itself in decades for the effective enlistment of a majority of the American public in the once lonely struggle to protect our heritage and to preserve for unborn generations of Americans and Canadians the kind of homogeneity of visual environment, the "sense of place," that we have all so often cherished abroad.

# ICCROM
## An International Clearinghouse and Training Centre

CEVAT ERDER

The increase in concern for our material cultural heritage and the intensification of efforts to preserve irreplaceable elements for the enrichment of the lives of all people have become so pervasive that we can feel justifiably optimistic about the future.]Yet it was not until the nineteenth century that a general cry went up for common action to safeguard the character of cities, their buildings and their streets, as well as their environment. The growth of cities, especially the proliferation of new road systems and of high-rise development affecting the pattern and scale of the existing urban fabric, has led in recent years to a significantly higher degree of concern for environmental values.

As a result thousands of organizations at the local, regional, and national level and millions of people work for heritage preservation today. They are fighting to save innumerable buildings, historic quarters, ancient cities, archaeological ruins, and areas of natural beauty from permanent destruction. To this end they are compiling inventories; initiating research; creating new museums; rewarding successful conservation projects; publishing books; making films; organizing exhibitions; offering training courses, summer camps and study tours; passing new laws; and strengthening existing organizations or setting up new ones.

We can rightly feel that conservation is no longer something special—a luxury to be dispensed with when times get hard or economic development demands the contrary. This concern for conservation, shared today by governments and many private individuals, made its first major appearance at the international level towards the end of the nineteenth century. The Hague conventions on protection against the damages of armed conflict are clear indications of this concern. The first criteria or guiding principles for the effective conservation of historic monuments appeared almost at the same time. The meeting of the International Union of Architects, which took place in Madrid in 1904, had a separate section devoted to the classification of historic buildings and the criteria to be applied to the protection of monuments. These included a precise statement that this was a specialized field that needed to be handled by technicians and architects trained specifically in conservation and holding officially recognized diplomas.

Among the products of this concern at the international level is the International Centre for the Study of the Preservation and the Restoration of Cultural Property, created by Unesco in Rome in 1959. The principal functions of ICCROM, as it is popularly known, are to collect, study, and circulate documentation concerned with scientific and technical problems of the preservation and restoration of cultural property; to coordinate, stimulate, or institute research in this domain; to give advice and make recommendations on general or specific points; and finally to assist in training research workers and technicians in raising the standard of restoration work.

At the time of its founding twenty-five years ago, ICCROM had only nine member states. It now has seventy-three, as well as sixty associate members—important public and private institutions concerned with conservation and training in various parts of the world.

This success may serve to indicate the distinctive character of ICCROM's work, resulting from the practical slant given to its research and from its constant concern with the possibilities of applying this research. But it is also indicative of the increasing concern around the world with preservation issues, together with the increasing number of agents threatening to damage and destroy cultural property.

In its work ICCROM tries to combine advanced technologies with traditional techniques as the need arises. In twenty-five years of practical experience it has been able to demonstrate that it is possible to protect historic monuments using techniques that are not only both simple and effective, but are accessible to many countries possessing only limited resources. A number of examples of this type have been mentioned in *Appropriate Technologies in the Conservation of Cultural Property,* published by Unesco in 1981. For further examples it is worthwhile consulting the publications of the National Research Laboratory for Conservation of Cultural Property, Lucknow, India.

ICCROM's major means of diffusing this knowledge, apart from the collection of scientific and technical data, is through its training programmes. This is certainly the most effective way to make available to experts in all branches of restoration work, from craftspersons to

Ellora Caves, India. Joint ICCROM/Archaeological Survey of India workshop on new techniques in the conservation of mural paintings.

scientists, the widest possible range of new knowledge and techniques required for the protection of cultural property. Each year ICCROM provides courses lasting from four to six months in Rome on the scientific principles of conservation, the conservation of buildings and sites, the conservation of mural paintings, and a shorter course on preventive conservation in museums. In addition ICCROM organizes courses in various parts of the world, including a series of training programmes on specific areas such as wood in Norway, stone in Venice, adobe in Peru, mural painting in Thailand, and climate and lighting control in museums in London, Dublin, Los Angeles, and Caracas.

We would draw your attention here to the fact that while training of conservation specialists and technicians is a worldwide problem, it is more acute in the Third World. A recent study carried out by ICCROM showed that the vast majority of training centres are located in Europe. These number some fifty training schools or institutes for restorers, as against only eighteen in the rest of the world. Of the overall total, those catering to architect-restorers number over twenty in Europe as against thirteen in the rest of the world.

Bearing this in mind, ICCROM is carrying out a programme of

collaboration with all concerned international organizations aimed at devising national programmes in cooperation with member states and at establishing a worldwide network of training centres through the setting up of national, regional, or subregional institutes.

As a scientific and technical organization, ICCROM's concern for training and for the development and distribution of didactic materials was confirmed by the recommendations of experts from different parts of the world who met in Rome in December 1982 under the auspices of Unesco and the International Council on Monuments and Sites (ICOMOS). During this meeting, it was observed with a certain satisfaction that the teaching of architectural conservation has developed in a number of countries. Yet it was also noted that the general evolution of mankind has led to such a broadening of the concept of cultural heritage and such an acceleration of the process of revitalization that conservation work is often entrusted to poorly trained technicians or even to technicians with no specific training at all. Thus the problem of education becomes ever more acute and in need of a solution.

After reviewing the curricula of existing courses, those attending this meeting found it necessary to point out that "specialization in architectural conservation requires the harmonious integration of the historical, humanistic (defining the bases and aims of conservation), scientific, technical and economic aspects, the latter providing the means required for practical solutions." Since the complex nature of architectural conservation renders it of necessity "a multidisciplinary activity in which, according to each individual case, the architect, the engineer, the archaeologist, the urban planner, the art historian, the economist, the social scientist, etc., must collaborate, it is also to be recommended that the specialists, in the various disciplines involved, be encouraged to exchange views and that some form of training in conservation be given to those specialists in order to facilitate interdisciplinary collaboration based on a common methodology."

ICCROM, which on the one hand acts as a clearinghouse for scientific research and information and, on the other, promotes research and the application of modern techniques in the conservation field, uses its training programmes to diffuse this concept. The basic concept guiding all training at ICCROM was described by my predecessor, Dr. Bernard Feilden, as being roughly a combination of the essence of the "Standards of Practice and Professional Relationships for Conservators" adopted by the International Institute for Conservation American Group Committee on Professional Standards and Procedures (New York, June 8, 1963) and the "Code of Ethics for

Sechin, Peru, advisory mission. Adobe monuments are inspected to make recommendations for their consolidation and protection.

Art Conservators," together with the "Venice Charter" promoted worldwide by ICOMOS.

The Venice Charter was unanimously approved at the Second International Congress of Architects and Technicians of Historic Monuments in 1964. One of the members of the drafting committee, Professor Paul Philippot, was at that time the director of ICCROM. In the charter, the concept of the historic monument was reconsidered and expanded. To the monumentality of the single structure were added visual extensions encompassing urban and rural settlements. We are no longer dealing only with "great works of art but also with more modest works which have acquired cultural significance with the passing of time."

Thus both a profound understanding of cultural problems and a wide range of specialized technical skills are required to deal with the complexity of an architectural and environmental whole, created over a period of time, involving human and natural factors and the generally fragile conditions of its structure and materials.

Article 2 of the Venice Charter, placed at the beginning of the document in the section devoted to definitions, is a sound one. It states that "the conservation and restoration of monuments must have recourse to all the sciences and techniques which can contribute to the study and safeguarding of the architectural heritage." This statement is clarified and strengthened by Article 10: "Where traditional techniques prove inadequate, the consolidation of a monument can be achieved by the use of any modern technique for conservation and construction, the efficacy of which has been demonstrated by scientific data and proved by experience."

These articles both reflect a fairly tardy admittance of the participation of science and technology in conservation. And rightly so. Earlier attempts by scientists to interfere with the conservation of antiquities had not been very successful, and it took some time before this situation improved. Gradually scientists, realizing the difficulties involved in practical conservation work, diverted their efforts to a less dangerous area—that of the analysis of artifacts. Very often scientists are interested in the value of the past, but concern for the future of these objects is seldom evident. Of course, the contribution of science and modern materials to modern conservation practice is undeniable, but this has been proven and justified only by the conservator who uses them.

The adaptation of scientific concepts and ideas to conservation practice has parallels in other branches of technology. The technologist who is trying to translate laboratory data into efficient processes has a tedious life, and perhaps even more so in conservation practice. Some of the many variables involved in conservation, such as social, aesthetic, and historic values, lie more often than not outside the field of competence of any scientist. In addition, the outcome of conservation processes is judged by a customer (a historian, an architect or, very often, a lay person) who usually knows very little about scientific and technical processes but does know what he wants. The difficulty of obtaining an objective evaluation and the necessity of allowing a fair amount of time to pass before being able to judge the final results of a conservation process can cause scientists to be reluctant to become involved in practical conservation. The true scientist's concept of time and that of a conservationist are quite different.

Nevertheless it is not surprising to find scientists who are attracted by this subject. Primarily they find the objects to be conserved fascinating; second the conservation field offers a variety of new avenues in the sphere of application. These two factors together induce the scientist to become involved emotionally. He then automatically throws himself from start to finish into the task of saving objects of historical value. The same attitude can be observed among those conservators who are not always content with the slow process

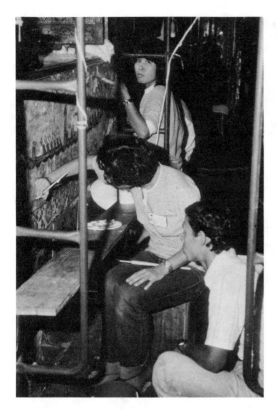

Wat Phra Kaew, Chapel of the Emerald Buddha, Royal Palace, Bangkok, Thailand. Demonstration of reintegration techniques.

of a sound testing procedure and the services of technologists. They tend to undertake themselves the entire cycle of operations from testing to application and final evaluation. Both approaches are undoubtedly questionable. "Multidisciplinary" is a word often voiced but seldom applied; we should constantly bear in mind that conservation, with so many variable components, can not progress without an efficient, well-balanced interdisciplinary approach.

We would like to define conservation as a developing branch of science supported by many disciplines but coordinated in one single theory, and it is on this basis that ICCROM is carrying out its mandate.

We maintain that poverty and the destruction of cultural property do not always go hand in hand. Developing countries are excellent examples of this, and many individual cases might be cited, such as the simultaneous development of welfare and the increase in destruction in the Middle East. Just as conservators should be armed with scientific and technological aids in order to perform their function

Florence, Italy. ICCROM sent teams to Venice and Florence to participate
in the massive volunteer effort to save the treasures of these cities
immediately after the 1966 floods.

properly, so scientists should have at their service a properly equipped
laboratory. However, a country may become rich and have the most
luxuriously equipped research laboratories in the conservation field,
but this alone will never guarantee that quality restoration work will
be carried out.

Indeed our activities at ICCROM are tempered by the realities of
scientific and technical, as well as financial and environmental resources. It is understood that simple techniques that have been soundly
tested and appropriately selected are generally better than risky
interventions using new, untested materials; yet applied science has
a crucial role to play in supplementing traditional techniques in cases
where these have failed to counter the increasing damage caused by
atmospheric pollution and/or vibrations. We urge the efficient maintenance of historic buildings and museums and their consolidation
against earthquakes. We tend to advise examination of the various
lines of action possible, given the natural environment of the monuments, in order to arrive at a proper selection of the least harmful
course, bearing in mind at all times that minimum intervention is
always best. Each project must have a clearly defined objective; costly
confusion must absolutely be avoided.

If we accept the definition of conservation as a new, developing science, we should realize that this definition can only be a modest one. We will need to secure aid from fields outside our competence and work with scientists and nonscientists of different disciplines, if we want to remain in this pioneering, but enormously stimulating and fascinating profession.

# Evolving
# Concepts
# and Practices

# Architectural Conservation
## *The Triumph of an Idea*

STEPHAN TSCHUDI-MADSEN

Restoration is a truly vast and challenging subject. Should it be tackled on a world scale? Over thousands of years? Confronted with such a vast field, I think the first thing to do is to dig into the etymology of the word *restoration* itself. The word *restaurateur,* in continental Europe at least, can still indicate either the slightly corpulent gentleman who greets you at the entrance of his little restaurant or the bespectacled specialist in a white laboratory coat making the lightest retouch with his squirrel-tail brush on a seventeenth-century painting. This double meaning of the word can be traced back to the eighteenth century. In 1765 a baker opened an eating house in the Rue des Poulies in Paris. The following evangelical inscription was placed above the entrance: "Venite ad me omnes qui stomacho laboratis, et ego vo restaurabo" (Come to me all who suffer in the stomach and I will restore you). This is said to have been the first restaurant, and the use of the word in this sense became common from then on.

But as far back as the sixteenth century, the word *restaurant* was also used to mean repair. In the *Dictionnaire de l'ancienne langue francaise* (1902) we find "faire un restorant d'une table de rubis pour nostre nepvew le prince de Danemarcque."

What is the original stem of the word *restore* and what could the etymological explanation be? The Indo-European root *st(h)a* means "stand." This has an extension with *u/v* and *r,* and in the Greek *stavros,* which means something standing, a pole or a stake. *Staur* in Latin means to "strengthen, make fast." This meaning certainly coincides well with the Indo-European original stem *st(h)a*—stand. To make a long linguistic excursion very short, *staurare* means "fasten, strengthen the poles or stakes"—the stavros. With the prefix *re,* again, *restaurare* in Latin thus means "restrengthening the poles." Here we have reached the solution: in military architecture, as far back as we can follow written sources and archaeological evidence, there has always been ample use of poles and stakes as fences or supporting elements.

*Restaurare*, in modern English *restore*, thus means to "restrengthen the fortifications"—actually to *repair* them. The term "to restore" obviously very soon acquired the general meaning "to repair," and thus the word lived on through the centuries—even in the sense of repairing the stomach!

Samuel Johnson in his famous *Dictionary of the English Language* (1755) simply states that *restoration* is "the act of replacing in a former state. To give back what has been lost or taken away." It was only in the nineteenth century that the meaning of the word started to change, this time away from the notion of repair, or at least moving towards the idea of a special sort of repair. The romantic movement brought a new dimension to the idea. Given the movement's retrospective enthusiasm, mediæval cathedrals and castles were examined and came into focus—both for good and for ill.

In 1866 the greatest restoring architect of all, Viollet-le-Duc, gave the classic definition of restoration: "To restore a building is to reestablish it to a completed state which may never have existed at any particular time." This way of thinking obviously left a good deal of room for fantasies. By the mid-nineteenth century, "restoration" had become a mania. Old parts of buildings were pulled down and new ones erected in a better and more "correct" style. The architects themselves decided what the past should look like.

The outstanding French antiquarian Prosper Mérimée reflects a further change in the understanding of the notion. He says in his *Rapport sur la restauration de Notre-Dame de Paris* (1845): "Par restauration nous entendons la conservation de ce qui existe et la reproduction de ce qui a manifestement existé. (By restoration we understand the conservation of that which exists and the recreation of that which has definitely existed.) By now "restoration" has become "conservation." This is an important change.

It was in England, however, that the reaction was strongest. Ruskin lashed out against restoration in the chapter "The Lamp of Memory" in *The Seven Lamps of Architecture* (1849): "Restoration, so called, is the worst manner of Destruction . . . Restoration is always a lie. . . . " In 1862 the architect G. G. Scott "almost could wish the word *restoration* expunged from our architectural vocabulary." In 1877 restoration was compared with measles. In 1879 William Morris described it as "wholesale destruction," and in 1880 it was seen as a euphemism for destruction. In 1884 the word itself had become "odious," and in 1891 restoration was seen as "a fallacy and an impossibility."

In our century we have adopted Prosper Mérimée's view that conservation is the goal. Ruskin said the same about the monuments:

"We have no right to touch them. They are not ours." We might even speak of a "New Ruskinism" that reflects the utmost carefulness in dealing with historic monuments or ruins.

In order to sum up this etymological survey, leading from the Greek *stavros* to the New Ruskinism of today, I would like to quote the French writer A. N. Didrot who as early as 1839 said: "When it comes to ancient monuments, it is better to consolidate than to repair, better to restore than to rebuild, better to rebuild than to embellish; in no case should anything be added, and above all nothing be taken away." This epigrammatic formula has been repeatedly quoted, until it turns up in abbreviated form as an American maxim: "Better to preserve than to repair, better to repair than restore, and better to restore than reconstruct" (O. M. Bullock, "The Restoration Manual," Connecticut, 1966).

## De Monumentum ad Naturam

With this short linguistic and etymological introduction, we should now be able to talk more precisely about our subject. It will enable us in particular to consider how, from the romantic period up to our own day, restoration has developed from the preservation of the single monument, to the preservation of monuments in their sur-roundings, to the preservation of groups of buildings in nature—and even to nature itself.

This development has had at least three stages: first, interest in the single building under the responsibility of a single individual; next, an interest in conserving various types of monuments and their surroundings with public support; finally, preservation of whole groups of monuments in a wide environmental context.

### The Single Monument and the Single Individual

Let us then start with the first stage of our development: the single individual coming to the rescue of the single monument. I have chosen three examples—a French castle, a Norwegian stave church, and an English cathedral.

What could be better to choose as a first example than Viollet-le-Duc's restoration of Pierrefonds for the Emperor Napoleon III? Of course one could have chosen Viollet-le-Duc's restoration of the Cathedral of Vézelay, which is a foundation stone in French and indeed in European restoration history. Rightly, it is now one of the French monuments on the World Heritage List.

The restoration of Pierrefonds, however, has a more romantic flavour. The castle is situated in the Forest of Compiègne, north of Paris, and was built by Louis d'Orléans at the end of the fourteenth century. It is regarded as one of the finest representations of mediæval military architecture. It was also a secret meeting place in the struggle against Louis XIII, and Richelieu gave the order that it should be completely demolished. But the castle's robust mediæval construction resisted these efforts, and it was never completely destroyed. It remained in its partly ruined state for two centuries until the Empress Eugénie, fascinated by this mediæval monument—and by the young architect Viollet-le-Duc—decided to make it her hunting castle. She decided to pay the costs of restoration entirely out of her own pocket, and in 1857 Viollet-le-Duc presented his first sketches, including the keep and two other towers. In 1862 restoration of the exterior was finished—so successfully that Eugénie decided to complete the work by restoring the interiors as well.

Viollet-le-Duc was at first reluctant, but convinced by both the money available and the forceful imperial charm, he set out to produce a masterpiece in restoration. We might say of him as Victor Hugo said of Walter Scott: "He forced us to recognize what we have never seen." Thus the restoration of Pierrefonds is a classic example of how an individual—or two—takes an interest in restoration, carries it through, and pays for it—all for the benefit of the very few.

In a northern corner of Europe, strangely enough, such ideas were catching on at the same time as in France, Germany, and England. I. C. Dahl, a Norwegian painter trained in Germany, had become familiar with the most advanced preservation ideas as early as the 1830s. After extensive travels in Europe, he discovered that his native country had an architectural heritage that existed nowhere else—the stave churches. These wooden buildings, with their unique vertical construction, were endangered by lack of maintenance and by a developing society. Although no such buildings were to be found in the rest of Europe, in Norway they were pulled down at the rate of one every third year. This was due to the poverty of Norway—the same poverty that had originally preserved the churches because of lack of funds to build anything more modern.

In 1836 Dahl published a book on the stave churches, *Denkmale einer sehr ausgebildeten Holzbaukunst aus den frühsten Jahrhunderten in den inneren Landschaften Norwegens*. It must have been very frustrating for a European-minded intellectual to see his compatriots destroy what he knew was unique. He therefore engaged himself in the struggle for the preservation of these buildings. One particular

**Heddal stave church, Telemark, Norway.**
*(Photo: Royal Norwegian Ministry of Foreign Affairs, Oslo, Norway.)*

example—the Vang stave church from the twelfth century—is typical, I think. The congregation at Vang wanted a bigger and better church, and Mr. Dahl wanted to preserve the old one. He made several suggestions, among them that the church be moved to the King's garden in the capital. Finally he bought it himself, tired of offering it to everybody "as a pot of sour beer," as he used to say. Later the church was taken over by the King of Prussia and moved to East Prussia in 1842, where it still stands in a somewhat reduced state.

Several stave churches were saved in this period, and again I think it is typical that this was due to the enthusiastic individual, to the pioneer, who so often carried the financial burden himself. The rest of the nation was asleep.

The most controversial of all restorations in England was that of Salisbury Cathedral; the project occupies a pivotal position not only in the history of English restoration and conservation but in the history of European conservation as a whole. This is partly because the work was directed by an architect of considerable stature, and partly because it was done in such a radical way. The main reason, however, is the fervent criticism it aroused, criticism that reflects essential attitudes towards restoration during that period: restoring versus preservation—*l'unité de style* versus diversity in style. The architect was James Wyatt, who earned himself several nicknames in the course of the restoration: "Wyatt the destroyer," "Wyatt the Vandal," and "Wyatt the Villain."

Wyatt inspected the cathedral in 1787, and in 1789 the work—initially a much needed renovation—began. Two late mediæval chapels were removed, as were the seventeenth-century reredos. The altar was moved, and nearly all the important tombs. The murals were scraped down, and the stained glass windows were subjected to a similar fate.

Criticism was voiced by both architects and clergymen. One man, a certain John Carter, wrote no less than 212 articles against the restoration in *Gentleman's Magazine* (in a not very gentlemanly style!). Books were written about the restoration. About the altar it was said that "it has evidently more appearance of a toilet than of a communion-table. . . . The choir was transformed to a portico."

Two things are especially interesting in this case. First, Wyatt is reproached not so much for the additions he made but for what he removed from the cathedral. This proves the emotional aspect of restoration, especially in churches. Second, we recognize the rigour of the *l'unité de style* principle.

There are several English examples of additions adapted to the original architecture. Both Christopher Wren and Inigo Jones showed great respect when they approached Gothic monuments. But James Wyatt introduced the "correct" Gothic style in his attempt to obtain unity. He introduced "uniformity into the sacred edifice"—he wished to "reduce each cathedral to a single room," as one critic put it.

Naturally the restoration of the Château de Pierrefonds cannot be compared with the restoration of Salisbury Cathedral (so much was added to the one, so much removed from the other) but in our context we can observe that both restorations reflect the dominance of the single individual and the needs of the few. Furthermore, we are confronted with the *l'unité de style* principle that came to dominate nearly all restorations throughout the nineteenth century.

*The National Need*

We now proceed to the next step in the development of restoration. During the latter half of the nineteenth century, the interest that different countries had in preservation was organized and more or less nationalized. This was closely related to legislation, which required that a responsible body be put in charge of heritage protection work. Italy introduced legislation in 1872, Spain in 1873, Hungary and

A splendid example of an early eighteenth-century merchant's mansion in Stavanger in Norway's Fjord Country. *(Photo: Norwegian National Tourist Office.)*

Egypt in 1877, England in 1882, Finland in 1883, Turkey in 1884, France in 1887, and Romania in 1892, to mention only a few. By the beginning of the twentieth century, most European nations had organized their own national protection system.

Around the turn of the century, the German-speaking countries began to join the leaders in the fields of art history and restoration philosophy, with scholars such as W. Frodl and A. Riegl. They had been restoring just as much and in just the same way as the rest of Europe, but ideas such as *Alterswert* (age value) came to the fore.

A whole new anthropological interest began to develop as well. Restoration was no longer the ideal—conservation was. A new range of interests was presented to the conservationists. To use William Morris's words in a letter to Ruskin, " . . . to my mind it would be worth the trouble, and years of our little society's (SPAB) life, if we could save one little gray building in England" (May 26, 1880). It was no longer only castles and manor houses but the homes of ordinary people that were to be saved. In this field the Scandinavian countries were leading the way in the 1890s with the Open Air Museum and the folk museums, where buildings and the ways and means of life of the ordinary farmer and craftsperson and even poorer people were preserved and displayed. As one of the pioneers, Anders Sandvig, put it in 1905, "In my opinion the museums should be collections of homes, where it is possible to come close to the people who lived in them. . . . Not only the big farm with its many buildings . . . but also the homes of the small farmers and the crofters, the craftsman's cottage up on the hill, and the outfarm deep in the forest." A conscious social profile gave a new dimension to conservation work. Irreversibility, truthfulness, the object and the monument as an historic document, the equalizing of periods, and proper documentation were among the new ideas and guiding principles.

In the first decades of the twentieth century, more recent buildings were included from different social levels. Old quarters, such as Williamsburg in the United States, where restoration work started in 1928, were significant additions, and preservation of entire historic towns also achieved recognized status. The need to preserve had in many cases entered national consciousness and began to overlap with nationalistic ideas. Then came the world wars. Destruction during World War I was terrible in many parts of Europe. The ravages of the second were many times worse and more widespread. They made it even more vital to maintain the material fabric of continuity between past and present.

As the people of Warsaw, Leningrad, Coventry, Dresden, and many other cities began anew after the guns had fallen silent, they showed a strongly renewed interest in rebuilding their old cities. It was not the interest in the single monument, but *the monument as a national symbol* that was necessary to restore. It was not only old churches but entire old towns, not only palaces but ordinary places. It was a question of national identity, and it grew to a national need—a need to establish cultural continuity by preserving the past. This national urge is easy to understand. In eastern European countries it is clear that the preservation of the past has a more important place in the life of a nation. There are several reasons for this: more was destroyed here; the socioeconomic systems are more nationally centralized; traditions of craftsmanship are more alive; and, finally, political realities reflect the need to preserve a special and national heritage.

Warsaw is a classic example. During World War II, 782 of its 957 historic buildings were completely demolished, 141 partly destroyed, and only 34 left unharmed. The Old Town and marketplace were left in ashes and ruins. For those who returned in 1945, an ashtray or a teaspoon, a jug or a doorhandle that had miraculously survived the war, were the dearest treasures of their owners. "Not because of their value, for they had none, but because of their emotional meaning," writes Adolf Ciborowski in *Warsaw: A City Destroyed and Rebuilt* (Warsaw, 1969, p. 278).

Because of these emotional feelings, the Old Town was the first place to be cleared. It was rebuilt over ten years, using as documentation the famous paintings by the eighteenth-century Italian painter Canaletto, photographs, and, most important, the records and measurements made by students of Polish architectural history in the Department of Architecture at the Warsaw Polytechnic. Most of the reconstructed buildings were destined for housing purposes. As far as possible they were given modern facilities. More daylight was provided by removing outhouses and also by reducing the depth of the buildings wherever the historians had no objection.

It was clear to all that the territory of Poland "must be recreated to be passed on to coming generations," and as Ciborowski continues: "That is the reason for a decision unprecedented in the theory of restoration of historic areas and buildings." This is certainly true, and Warsaw recreated must be seen to be believed. Yet as in any restoration there will always be critical remarks. The most typical I have heard was that of the expert who found the reconstruction all too dry and correct. "It all lacks the smell of garlic," he said. It all depends on the eye . . . or the nose.

Equally unbelievable is the reconstruction of the Royal Castle, specially rebuilt in the eighteenth century and completely flattened in 1944. Before it was totally destroyed, both specialists and the "man in the street" managed to save pieces or ornaments, parts of profiles, bits of textiles, so that not only the whole building but all the interiors could be meticulously reconstructed. In 1971 a civic committee for the reconstruction of the Royal Castle was founded. In 1974 the walls were reconstructed, and after the interiors had been completely redone by teams of skilled craftsmen, the castle was reopened. Time and peace will make the new castle what the old one used to be: a proud proof of the past.

Another example should be briefly mentioned because it reflects some of the same ideas. During the same war, the pearl of Leningrad palaces, Petershof, built by Rastrelli in 1749–56, was completely destroyed. As soon as the war was over reconstruction began, and fortunately old drawings of the statues existed. In 1960 the gardens were restored as well as the walls and roofs of the palace. Today there is no trace of the former destruction.

The same point can be made in a more peaceful context. The

restoration—or reconstruction—of the northernmost of the European Gothic cathedrals was born of the wish of a small nation, Norway, to link its rather poor present to a rich past. The west front of the medieval cathedral was begun in 1248, and the grandeur of the cathedral must have been even more impressive than in the rest of Europe, since the city was largely made up of small one- and two-storey wooden houses. By the seventeenth century, however, only the choir, transept, and the lower part of the west front were left standing. The movement for national political and cultural freedom from Sweden came to a head in 1905 with Norway's independence. After a hundred years of reconstruction and restoration (from 1869 to 1969), the cathedral finally was "replaced in its former state," as Samuel Johnson would have put it.

Architecturally this work is to be regarded from the same point of view as the restoration of Pierrefonds or Salisbury or the many German, English, and French Gothic cathedrals. But it was not a one-man show. Rather it was the wish of a whole nation, based on deeper national feelings linked to a consciousness of and a need for the past. From this historical and philosophical point of view it belongs to the second phase of the development of restoration.

## Nature and the Global Perspective

We proceed to the third stage with Major James Savage and his battalion of voluntary golddiggers. When these adventurers were fighting their way through the wildest mountain area of the Sierra Nevada in the autumn of 1851, a vast valley suddenly unfolded before them. It impressed them with its beauty but hardly softened their hearts: the battalion's aim was to wipe out the Uzumati Indians. Savage and his men were among the very first white people to see this panorama and behold this valley, the home country of the Uzumatis, from which the name Yosemite is derived.

Since then the beauty of the Yosemite Valley has remained un-changed. The enormous mountain ranges, El Capitan, The Three Brothers, and Half Dome, drop steeply in mighty thrusts down towards the idyllic valley where the Merced River twines itself through the sand, surrounded by green fields and a thousand-year-old forest where bears and deer still roam.

Yosemite is characteristic of the distinctive quality of heritage conservation in America, with its integration of the natural environ-ment right from the start. Such an outlook on nature was unknown in Europe. To be sure the royal forests in many countries were well protected, but when the King of Bavaria in 1805 decided to protect a magnificent oak tree in the northern part of Bavaria, it was looked upon as a curiosity. There was also a special reason why Napoleon III sought to preserve the splendid trees in the Fontainebleau forest— the wish to protect the dearest motifs of the Barbizon school from disappearing. In America, however, the protection of nature was based on the need for beauty and recreation. The United States has been the leader in this field, and the principle of active state-supported conservation of nature has gradually gained ground elsewhere.

Unesco's 1972 convention concerning the Protection of the World Cultural and Natural Heritage, usually referred to as the World Heritage Convention, codifies the principles of heritage conservation as the shared responsibility of humanity. It makes a significant innovation in linking together what were traditionally regarded as two quite different sectors: the protection of the cultural heritage and of the natural heritage. It also introduces the specific notion of a "world heritage" whose importance transcends all political and geographical boundaries.

In Article I of the World Heritage Convention we read first about "monuments," then "groups of buildings"; these are the two first stages outlined above. Sites are defined next as "works of man or the combined works of nature and of man, and areas including archaeological sites which are of outstanding universal value. . . . " In Article II we find reference also to "natural features consisting of physical and biological formations or groups of such formations which are of outstanding universal value for the aesthetic or scientific point of view." Thus a global and interdisciplinary approach prevails; this marks the triumph of the third stage in the development of preservation and points far into the future. Today 89 countries have ratified the convention and 216 sites are already on the World Heritage List, which expands each year by twenty to thirty monuments or sites.

Some of the sites mentioned are: the pyramid fields from Giza to Dahsur; the Cathedral of Aachen in Germany; L'Anse aux Meadows National Historic Park in Canada; the Palace and Park of Versailles and the Cathedral of Vézelay in France; the Historic Centre of Rome; Grand Canyon National Park and Independence Hall in America; and Cracow and Auschwitz Concentration Camp in Poland. Less well-known sites include the Ngorongoro Conservation Area in Tanzania; the Plitvice Lakes National Park in Yugoslavia; the Buddhist ruins at Takht-i-Bahi and Sahr-i-Bahlol in Pakistan; and a stave church in Norway.

Yes, we have attained a truly global perspective and learned that

# The Common Heritage of the Americas
## Regional Cooperation

ROBERTO ETCHEPAREBORDA

Although the criteria of restoration possess an intrinsic worldwide unity, the preservation of the heritage of the Americas nevertheless requires certain approaches that differ from those used in other regions of the world. The hemisphere is a gigantic crucible of cultures whose patrimony derives from the remotest as well as the most recent past and is in a state of permanent synthesis.

Soon after it was formed in 1890, the Union of American Republics began to seek ways to meet the challenge of continued deterioration and pillaging of its cultural, archaeological, and historical patrimony. Because it is the oldest regional system in existence today, these antecedents are of particular interest.

At its Second International American Conference in Mexico in 1902, the Union began its first moves towards the protection of the common heritage of the Americas. Indeed if we examine the historical background of the different international American conferences up to 1948 and the creation of the Organization of American States (OAS), we find several important statements establishing the approach of the American republics towards a common response to heritage protection. Many efforts were made to establish treaties between countries; these involved not only what may be called protection against war as in the Roerich Pact adopted at Lima in 1938, but also the establishment of the first steps towards the protection of the pre-Columbian heritage of these nations.

It was not until the mid-1960s, however, that the inter-American system began to look more closely at the problems arising from threats to its heritage. In 1965 the First Pan American Symposium on Preservation and Restoration of Historical Monuments, sponsored by the OAS, was held in the city of Saint Augustine, Florida, in the United States. Yet its conclusions, like those of other bodies or meetings, consisted of very general recommendations lacking either national or international response. It was only at the Meeting on the Preservation and Utilization of Monuments and Sites of Artistic and Historical Value, organized by the OAS in Quito, Ecuador, in 1967, that the transition from theory to practical action began to emerge.

Until that date, how could the Latin American situation be described? There were no guiding principles to follow with regard to protection and utilization of the cultural heritage. In most of the member states there were no official agencies or paragovernmental institutions responsible for the protection, preservation, and restoration of the archaeological, historical, and artistic heritage. Only a few countries had some of the necessary specialized human resources because they were the ones with the largest number of cultural assets. The methods, techniques, and equipment used in the preservation and restoration of cultural properties, as well as in archaeological research, were out of date or inadequate. Legislation protecting the cultural heritage was also out of date and deficient in both legal and administrative procedures for its application.

## The Quito Standards and Their Application

The principles laid down in the final report of the Quito meeting came to be known as the Quito Standards. In 1968 the fifth meeting of the Inter-American Cultural Council adopted the text and recommended the establishment of an inter-American programme for the protection and utilization of the cultural heritage based on the aims and criteria set out in the document. The latter defines the nature and significance of "monuments and sites of artistic and historical value" and goes on to prescribe specific legal, technical, and administrative measures for their protection in the contemporary context, including their "enhancement," their use as tourist attractions, the promotion of social involvement and civic action, etc. (The document specified: "To enhance the usability and value of a historic or artistic property is to provide it with the objective and environmental conditions that, without detracting from its nature, emphasize its characteristics and permit its optimum use. The enhancement should be construed to operate on the basis of a transcendent purpose. In the case of Latin America, this purpose would undoubtedly be to contribute to the economic development of the region.")

Since 1968 the OAS, through its Regional Cultural Development Programme, has worked actively to promote the application of the

Machu Picchu, Peru, the ancient Inca capital situated north of Cuzco, discovered in 1911. *(Photo: Unesco/R. Laurenza.)*

Quito Standards in the member states. It has sponsored and provided advice on the establishment or strengthening of official or paragovernmental technical agencies and institutions for the preservation and suitable utilization of the cultural heritage (for example, national institutes of culture, offices of cultural heritage and of inventory of cultural properties, cultural heritage administrations, and the like). It has also facilitated technical advisory services by experts from outside the hemisphere for the most immediate tasks of preservation and restoration, and trained national personnel in the Inter-American Centres on Restoration of Cultural Properties in Mexico, Panama, and Peru, as well as through special courses in Spain. It has endeavoured to promote the application of modern methods in preservation, restoration, and archaeological research by organizing and equipping services and laboratories. It has provided advisory services in the preparation of new laws and administrative provisions and encouraged the preparation and acceptance by member states of inter-American standards, such as the Convention on the Protection of the Archaeological, Historical, and Artistic Heritage of the American Nations (Convention of San Salvador).

Various OAS seminars and technical meetings have also identified and/or recommended practical measures such as the establishment of an emergency fund to facilitate rapid deployment of resources for monuments in imminent danger of disappearance; the training of craftspersons as auxiliary manpower for monument restoration; the inclusion of programmes for the preservation of the monumental heritage in international lending agencies' financial plans; the inclusion of specific funds in all public service works for the archaeological research and rescue work that may be necessary; and the dissemination of knowledge about the cultural heritage at school and community levels.

Joint OAS-Unesco action also reflects a growing mutual interest in cultural heritage projects, an interest that has developed from a simple exchange of information into effective cooperation in multinational projects. Joint missions have been carried out to determine the methodology to be used in inventorying cultural properties and to analyze the status of the cultural heritage appropriate for encouraging cultural tourism in the Central American countries. Intensive courses were given on the inventorying of cultural properties, in San José, and on the restoration of movable cultural properties, at the Inter-American Subregional Centre in Lima. These activities received support from the International Council on Monuments and Sites (ICOMOS), the United Nations Environment Programme (UNEP), and the United Nations Development Programme (UNDP). Technical assistance included staffing institutions and agencies responsible for preserving the cultural heritage and providing the equipment and instruments required for efficient professional work.

The OAS Project on the Protection of the Cultural Heritage has invested approximately six million dollars in technical assistance, training, and equipment; it has mobilized national counterpart funds several times that amount and also obtained important international contributions. Examples include: (1) Antigua Guatemala, where the initial help given by the OAS permitted the development of important restoration work carried out by the national agency, the National Council for the Protection of Antigua Guatemala; (2) the restoration works under way on the Jesuit Mission Ruins in Paraguay—a first phase of this project, that of Trinidad, has just been undertaken with the cooperation of Unesco, the government of Spain, and other institutions of that country; and (3) the work on New Seville in Jamaica, which combines efforts of the OAS, Unesco, the government of Spain, and the Inter-American Development Bank.

**Argentina. Portal of Saint Ignacio Mini Church.** *(Photo: Unesco/ICOMOS Argentina.)*

## Monuments and Tourism

The Quito Standards contain a separate section on "Monuments as Tourist Attractions."[11] This reflects the interaction, particularly strong in the region, between tourist travel and the monumental heritage, which has become a major component of the "travel plant" and therefore should be a major factor in all development plans.

The Quito Standards elaborate this principle as follows:

> *From the tourist standpoint exclusively, monuments are a fundamental part of the "plant" available for operating that industry in a given region, but the extent to which this monument can serve the use to which it is put will depend not only on its intrinsic value, that is, on its archaeological, historic, or artistic significance or interest, but on the attendant circumstances facilitating its proper utilization. Therefore, restoration in itself may not always be sufficient to ensure that a monument can be exploited and become part of the travel plant of a region. It may be just as necessary to undertake such other infrastructure works as a road to provide access to the monument or an inn to lodge the*

*visitors at the end of the day—all in keeping with the environmental*
*nature of the region.*

## CARIMOS Plan

At present the situation of the English-speaking member states, especially those that have recently joined the organization, is similar to that of the Latin American countries in the mid-1960s. Consequently actions to be taken with respect to them should be similar to those adopted two decades ago by the Latin American member states. These actions will be taken in a coordinated way in accordance with the Greater Caribbean Plan for Monuments and Sites (CARIMOS), already under way within the framework of activities in celebration of the five-hundredth anniversary of the discovery of America (1992).

The multinational project known as the CARIMOS Plan was launched in 1982. It is of special significance for the preservation of historical monuments and sites and for the development of tourism in the region. The project's general aims are to preserve, restore, and revitalize the monumental heritage of civilian buildings (including local architecture), military constructions, and religious buildings of historical and/or artistic interest that individually or as a group constitute historical centres in the member states of the Caribbean Basin, in relation to maintenance of the cultural identity of their people and to their appropriate use for the development of cultural tourism.

The project aims specifically to identify, investigate, and compile an inventory of that monumental heritage; to prepare projects for consolidation, restoration, enhancement of surroundings, revitalization, and utilization of those historical centres; to direct and supervise execution of the projects; to train personnel; and to publish the results of the research and work done.

The plan will culminate in the year of the celebration of the five-hundredth anniversary of the arrival of Christopher Columbus in the New World. The years from 1984 to 1987 are expected to see a continuation of inventory compilation; the execution of projects designed to enhance the existing built environment as part of a programme of social and economic development; the encouragement of the establishment of "historic centres" in view of their significance to the social and cultural life of a community; the study of those features that are an integrative factor in the Caribbean; and the promotion of technical cooperation between countries, institutions, and individuals.

The third stage, up to 1991, will then see the consolidation and amplification of the activities initiated in the previous stages; publicity for the work already completed; and the execution of specific projects, on a regional basis, in conformity with the various aims and goals of CARIMOS.

## Catalyzing Further Energies

The OAS Regional Cultural Development Program will continue to provide high-level technical advisory services, equipment and materials, and training and retraining opportunities. It will also pursue its efforts to promote the exchange of specialized experience and the harmonization of national laws on heritage preservation. Activities to this end will serve in themselves as a catalyst for two types of integrated cultural processes: on the one hand, interdisciplinary research that links the restored works to history, to society, and to the way of life that existed when they were built; and on the other, incorporation of the restored monument into the society as a whole, as a source of both spiritual inspiration and improved living conditions of the inhabitants in surrounding areas.

# Historic Preservation in the United States
## A Historical Perspective

MICHAEL L. AINSLIE

In providing a context for contemporary issues facing preservation in the United States, it is appropriate to offer a historical perspective on the evolution of the preservation movement and community in this country.

The beginnings of preservation in this country can be traced back to the middle of the last century. In 1850 the New York State government rescued George Washington's headquarters at Newburg, New York. In 1856 came the decision by the Carpenters Company to renovate Carpenters Hall, the site of the first Continental Congress in 1774. Shortly thereafter the Mount Vernon Ladies Association, chartered in 1858 and led by a prominent South Carolinian, moved to preserve and save Mount Vernon from demolition. In 1888 the Society for the Preservation of Virginia Antiquities was founded. It began with the preservation of Jamestown Island, and soon expanded its efforts to include cemeteries, historic houses, and monuments throughout Virginia.

Some characteristics of these early efforts are important. First they were generally voluntary efforts by private citizens rather than by government. They focused on individual homes and sites of our early historic figures. And—particularly important, I think—they focused much more on history and much less on architecture.

In the early part of this century two major events occurred, within five years of each other, that shaped preservation as we practice it today. In 1926 John Rockefeller made a decision to restore Colonial Williamsburg, and this became a model for restored villages throughout this country—Old Sturbridge Village, Mystic Village in Connecticut, Old Salem in North Carolina, and many others. There was a realization here that history involves more than individual shrines, that it involves the homes of more than just the most important figures in our history. There was also a new focus, an emphasis on interpretation, that would enable the visitor to see and feel how life was lived in an earlier time.

Equally important, these restored areas became centers of research—research on archaeology, and on historic fabric—that led to more accurately recreated sites and living patterns. Again private individuals and private dollars were the catalyst. The most important development, in my view, came about in 1931 when the first historic district and the first local government police power action to protect historic resources were established in Charleston, South Carolina, with the formation of the first Historic District in America. This local effort to save buildings *not* as museums but in their current use as homes and businesses and in the context of a city was perhaps the most pivotal change in broadening historic preservation in this country. It was also the first effort of a local government to use police power that had normally been reserved for zoning and planning issues to protect particular types of structures and sites.

The role of the federal government in our preservation movement also began in the 1930s. The National Register of Historic Places and the Historic American Building Survey—an effort to identify and record buildings significant to American life and culture—came about in the 1930s. This continued through the 1940s, and after World War II the National Trust was founded as a result of a major study that showed that a major proportion of those early documented buildings of the 1930s had already been lost through demolition. The National Trust was founded in 1949 based largely on the British model, although it has evolved in some very different ways from the National Trust in the United Kingdom.

The two purposes of our National Trust were to be a steward of nationally significant landmarks—individual buildings—and, very broadly stated, to facilitate public participation in historic preservation. Perhaps the most far-reaching change in historic preservation occurred in 1966 with the passage of the National Historic Preservation Act. The act expanded our National Register from simply *nationally* important properties, which I believe numbered about 1,500 on the register at that time, to properties and districts and sites of local and state significance—a change that may seem minor but has in fact led to a massive proliferation of sites, districts, and buildings considered significant. Today well in excess of 32,000 entries are on our National Register. Over 2,100 districts and collectively over 200,000 structures, representing perhaps a half of 1 percent of the built environment in this country, are now listed.

Another major change was the creation of a federal agency, the Advisory Council on Historic Preservation, to oversee the activities of other federal agencies and their programs, and to minimize and seek to mitigate or find alternatives to the adverse impact on historic resources.

Another important feature was the creation of matching grants— grants not only to our National Trust, which continue though at declining levels during the current administration, but also matching grants to state governments. This inaugurated a whole new role in federal partnership that continues and is in fact quite strong today; in this partnership the federal government *manages* the National Register but state governments do most of the work in surveying and planning for register nominations and listings. Under the recent tax changes, this increasingly includes state certification of appropriate historic rehabilitation under tax incentives.

Other trends in the 1960s and 1970s that clearly affected the strength and role of preservation in this country included the massive reaction against the demolition of cities for federal urban renewal and highway projects—a continuing difficulty for us. Some of our urban problems—for example the troubles of 1968—led to a growth in what we call "the neighborhood movement." The neighborhood movement in recent years, and *only* in recent years, has come to see historic preservation as one of the most constructive *planning* tools— ways of dealing with communities—that exist. Instead of being adversaries, as was the case some years ago, we have increasingly become partners in planning for preservation of historic inner-city communities.

The growth of the environmental movement in this country has in many ways assisted us in historic preservation. The increase in federal environmental regulations and of reviews that prevent or delay inappropriate projects—projects frequently involving demolition of historic structures—has been an important factor.

All of these factors have meant that preservation has moved from what was perhaps a more theoretical universe into a political and more realistic one, a world dealing with politics, with legislation, with regulation, and with federal agencies on a daily basis.

The 1970s brought one of the more positive and appropriate responses, as we realized that while the National Register now was a very large reservoir of properties, we still had very few tools to provide incentives for private investment. Most of these buildings—I believe over 95 percent of National Register properties—are privately owned. In 1976 we therefore passed a tax act that provided federal tax incentives for private investment in National Register property. That law was changed once, in 1978, and again in 1981 under a major change in the tax bill of this administration. The 1981 law provides major incentives including a 25 percent federal tax credit (for every dollar spent on a Certified Rehabilitation, twenty-five cents is *rebated*, not deducted) to the individual, partnership, or corporation that makes that investment.

This particular change in our tax law has had a major impact on the pattern of investment and the pattern of development in our cities. In fiscal year 1983 the National Park Service, which administers this program under the Secretary of the Interior, certified $2.2 billion of investment, in over 2,600 National Register properties. Clearly this is much more significant than the direct federal support that had earlier been in the range of $20 to $30 million. It is estimated that another amount in excess of $2.2 billion will be certified in 1984. Congress is not wondering, as it has often done in the past, about changing or eliminating these tax credits because they are working! So we are very actively involved in lobbying and in convincing Congress, using some of the kinds of educational efforts that Mme. Paradis discusses in her article. We have been taking leaders in Congress *to* the communities, their *own* communities, to let them see what is going on.

Another important development is the building of a major computer econometric model to show the impact of not only the federal subsidy provided by these tax credits but also the job creation, the local tax revenues resulting from properties that return to the tax roll, and the creation of housing units, which has been a dramatic consequence of these incentives. (Over 40,000 new housing units have come into existence under these tax credits, approximately half of which derived from buildings that were not previously in housing usage.) There has been a broad social impact as well.

Local preservation organizations have also grown significantly, and today the National Trust has over 2,500 local and state preservation organizations. This fact has altered and dramatically increased our service requirements for providing technical support, financial and organizational assistance, and fundraising advice to the many local bodies that are now increasingly the stewards of the heritage of their communities. I think this is one of the more significant differences from the British National Trust, which has continued in its excellent way to be a property-owning organization. We are increasingly a representative for hundreds of local organizations, many of which in turn are property-owning as well as advocacy organizations.

Let me turn quickly to four or five current issues and trends in preservation. Certainly one of the most important issues is how to support the preservation of tax-exempt buildings—buildings owned by governments, churches, and non-profit organizations that are not eligible for the credits I mentioned earlier. Under the current administration we have seen an elimination of grants to provide assistance to this type of building, and this is causing us problems all over the country. It has manifested itself recently in a bill in the New York State legislature that would exempt all religious structures from landmark status, making it illegal to landmark a religious structure in New York State. The bill grew out of the controversy surrounding the project of St. Bartholomew's Church on Park Avenue in New York City, which wished to tear down part of its National Landmark structure in order to make room for a sixty-story high-rise building.

We also face the problem of communicating with groups to whom preservation has not been an important issue—minority groups, urban ethnic groups, and groups in rural and farming communities. We are developing interesting new tools to alter this. In 1981 the Trust began a program of grants—what we call a venture capital fund—for neighborhood organizations in historic districts. This fund, called the Inner City Ventures Fund, now has over $25 million of rehabilitation under way in historic inner city neighborhoods in low- and moderate-income communities. It has attracted sponsorship from major corporations in this country.

We also face the continuing issue of how to develop effective working partnerships with conservation and archaeological organizations. Work with these natural area conservation groups is an underdeveloped field in our preservation activity.

In closing it must be said that the preservation community in this country continues to find itself with a broad and diverse set of challenges. This past year we litigated to preserve the Apollo launch tower, from which the first manned shot to the moon took off in Cape Canaveral. We succeeded in negotiating a settlement with NASA to preserve—or at least "preserve" for the next three years—this important part of our contemporary culture. In recent months the National Trust has received a bequest of $10 million for the purpose of bringing James Madison's home in Montpelier, Virginia, under our stewardship, and we continue to be involved in preserving great estates and some of the more important national landmarks in this country. We are involved at the same time in preserving housing and structures in Chinatown in San Francisco and also a four-hundred-house historic district known as the Longwood Historic District in the

# The Preservation of Haiti's National Heritage

ALBERT MANGONÈS

The formulation of a policy for the preservation of Haiti's National Heritage, as officially stated by the President of Haiti, is the result of a holistic approach, integrating all the various aspects of this heritage—natural and cultural—as essential categories of the nation's resources. Consequently the problems related to specific preservation projects have been assigned adequate priority in the National Development Plan.

Of course factors of vastly different importance have determined the government's priorities under the main headings of agricultural production, infrastructures and communications, education, natural resources, and employment.

All the major objectives, however, have been established with a view to creating regional poles of development whose purpose is to check the powerful attraction exerted by the capital city of Port-au-Prince and help stem the population exodus from the rural areas. The creation or the consolidation of income-generating activities in the provinces is considered a prerequisite for a successful and coherent national development plan.

The country has also experienced an alarming acceleration of environmental decay in recent decades, owing to inadequate and wasteful exploitation of our natural resources. The population "explosion" and a dramatic struggle for survival have aggravated deforestation and erosion, and massive migration to the cities has quickened the pace of chaotic urban expansion.

Simultaneously, the pressures of the rising cost of living have reinforced the trend toward illicit traffic of precious and irreplaceable cultural property.

In such a situation a laissez-faire attitude would be highly detrimental to the cause of a coherent national development policy. This is why the government has taken a resolute stand in stating that the problems of preservation of our national heritage must be accounted for in the formulation of the overall national development plan.

169

The Citadelle Henri,
Haiti. This titanic
fortress, atop a chain of
rugged mountains,
dominates the vast spaces
of the Plaine du Nord.
Twenty thousand men
toiled between 1805 and
1820 to erect this "first
monument to the black
man's freedom regained."

The project to restore the Citadelle, the Palace of Sans-Souci, and the Ramiers Site was initiated in 1973 through a joint program of the Haitian government and the Organization of American States (OAS). It is significant that the purpose of this preliminary stage of action was to establish an inventory of the technical measures required to halt the deterioration of this monumental ensemble as well as a master plan for restoration work, with particular reference to the implications of the project for the promotion of tourism.

Emphasis was squarely placed, however, on a comprehensive and multidisciplinary approach to the preservation, restoration, and integral development of the area within a national historic park planned to encompass the natural environment of the monuments. The entire project is based on uncompromising respect for internationally accepted criteria concerning the methods and principles of historical restoration. Furthermore the projected program of utilization of the renovated ensemble is designed to promote a spirit of cultural identity.

However, the project also aims to improve the environment and the living conditions of those who dwell nearby or within the limits of the national park's territory. On the national level, the project provides for the restoration of Haiti's most significant historical monuments. It also constitutes a special contribution to the development plan of the Department of the North, one of the vital territorial entities of the republic, where the government intends to invest a considerable amount of resources and services for industrial, agricultural, and tourist infrastructures.

Finally, at the international level the ultimate goal of the project is to create a center for an international festival of arts, sciences, and culture dedicated to the unity of human destiny. We are convinced that the Citadelle shall continue to stand for what it is: the first monument of modern times to the black race at last liberated from slavery, a monument to every person's unconditional right to be free.

To these ends, and in spite of serious economic restrictions, the government resolutely assumed the main financial responsibility for the restoration work. The project was officially inaugurated on October 8, 1977, with a special operational annual budget of $360,000 granted by the President to:

*1. Initiate all urgent action necessary to protect and consolidate the existing structures;*

*2. Establish gradual control over the utilization of the sites;*

*3. Proceed with the technical studies and establish a schedule of the works to be done;*

*4. Formulate the terms of reference for the study of the National Historic Park, its management, and the guidelines of a general policy for the protection of natural and historic values of the park and of the monuments.*

The tentative boundaries of the national park were established by presidential decree on August 19, 1978, creating the National Historic Park of "La Citadelle, le Palais Sans Souci et le Site des Ramiers." In spite of serious financial difficulties we have proceeded to formulate the main objectives of the park project, which are:

*1. The socioeconomic study of the local population living within the limits of the park (population distribution, family structures and income, tourism impact, health, literacy, etc.);*

**Carrying planks up the steep gradient leading to the Citadelle, 1984.**
*(Photo: ISPAN/Antonio Marcelli.)*

> *2. The study of an effective control of land use in the park, for the protection of the local ecology and the renewal of the traditional habitat;*
> *3. An inventory of the local flora and fauna and the study of a tropical botanical garden;*
> *4. The provision for the creation of a training center for traditional construction skills and the training of field specialists in restoration (carpenters, masons, archaeologists, etc.).*

Today, six years after the official inauguration, the project has reached the stage where accomplishments, errors, and failures, as well as future potentialities and difficulties, may be substantially evaluated.

It can be safely stated today that the Haitian government's option to assign priority status to the project was correct. In fact while it has gradually become more difficult for the government to maintain its projected national financial contribution to the operational budget of the project, it is significant that international financial support has remained unimpaired, as witnessed by the following:

*1. Assistance from the United Nations Development Programme (UNDP) amounting to approximately US$380,000, continued through 1982-83 and partly extended through 1984;*

*2. A grant from Unesco of US$67,683 assigned to the purchase of a specific quantity of specially weather-treated lumber for the restoration of the roof structure of the "Batterie Royale" and the floor beams of the "Batterie Coidavid";*

*3. A donation by the Kress Foundation (USA) of US$50,000 for the purchase of special material for the "mise hors d'eau" of the Citadelle, and the preparation of a promotional traveling exhibition of photographs and drawings of the restoration work in progress; and*

*4. An offer of a US$100,000 grant from the Federal Republic of Germany as a contribution to the cost of improvement work on the Sans Souci-Citadelle road.*

These positive and substantial manifestations of interest in the project from multilateral and bilateral institutions confirm the validity of the multidisciplinary approach used by ISPAN and Unesco for the study and the presentation of this restoration project. It should be noted that, while maintaining the focus on the transcendental cultural significance of the project, a deliberate emphasis has been placed on the legitimate promotional potentialities of the project for tourism, rural development, soil preservation and partial reforestation in the national park, and intensive labor input, as well as appropriate and traditional technology integration in building and restoration procedures.

We are certain, therefore, that this is truly a pilot project, unique in many ways, and that valuable experience may be drawn from our work. It is evident that our main handicap is the size of our national operational budget. It is of course very difficult to assess realistically the wisdom of the decisions fixing the distribution of the available resources to the different development projects of the government. However, we know that the decisionmakers agree with us that the cash flow assigned to the project is not sufficient.

We also feel the need for greater flexibility, which would make it possible for such projects to enjoy direct access to sources of financing that are, at present, too narrowly assigned to specific development projects such as road construction, tourist promotion, and appropriate technology utilization. Existing regulations do not facilitate the financing of specific actions under such headings if a project is primarily classified as a heritage preservation project. Yet it is evident that restoration projects of major scope have definite impacts on other

**The Palace of Sans-Souci.**

sectors of social, economic, and political importance. The investments required to save monuments like Mont-Saint-Michel, Versailles, Machu Picchu, or Borobudur, and the maintenance costs of these ensembles, may be impossible to justify from a strictly local cost-benefit analysis. But could there be any doubt as to the overall benefits generated on a broad spectrum for other national sectors by the successful realization of such cultural preservation projects?

As for Haiti's particular major cultural heritage preservation project for "Le Parc national historique de la Citadelle, du Palais Sans-Souci et du Site des Ramiers," it should be evident that the crucial difficulty we confront in presenting a credible argument for its "economic" merit—besides its indisputable cultural transcendence—is the insufficiency of our financial resources. The essential restoration alone would cost approximately US$4 million.

This amount, however, should be available within a period of two years. But the cost of the road construction, which is not, properly speaking, restoration work, should be met simultaneously from other financial sources. Here again the estimate is not very high: only US$700,000. However it is institutionally very difficult to ensure that this type of financing is assigned to a heritage preservation project.

These observations are probably applicable to many other heritage protection projects. We hope they will be helpful in working out new approaches to solving the problems involved. Those of us committed to the difficult task of protecting the common heritage of humanity need to be able to demonstrate that the investments required for the restoration of great national monuments can be, and often actually are, sound contributions to achieving the overall objectives of a national development plan.

# The Press and Cultural Heritage Preservation
## *A Canadian Perspective*

ANDRÉE G. PARADIS

Coming from the "Mystic North,"[1] I shall try with the help of the northern lights to approach the concept of cultural heritage in its broadest sense. The idea of a world cultural heritage is an important part of the phenomenon of universalization. Yet this broad concept, which represents progress in human awareness and a process of opening out to the whole world, meets with indifference if not resistance from the general public. The public is rarely well informed, not because the specialized press is inadequate in providing such information, but because only a small percentage of space and time is allotted by the communication media to information on cultural heritage problems and culture in general. There is little media time left after soap operas, news, religion, meteorology, and public and financial affairs, and that small fraction of time is given more to the performing arts than to the visual arts, literature, or heritage problems. Until this state of affairs is changed, the specialized press will be gravely limited in its mission of reaching out to a broad public so as to ensure the survival of the cultural heritage of humanity.

The present crisis of our cultural heritage, although not new in history, is linked to the radical crisis of modernity of the late 1950s and early 1960s: the dilemma of either restoring the past or searching for new formulas. The best results seem to have been obtained from a mixture of solutions. Yet there was a period during which all creative efforts seemed to favour a notion of modernity that rejected all past experience. Then the pendulum swung back, bringing with it a new wave of nostalgia for the past and a quest for its monuments and artifacts. Already in Vienna during World War I, artists, architects, musicians, and scientists sensed that renewal influenced by tradition could mean the rebirth of the languages of art, music, and architecture. Adolf Loos created a revolutionary style that makes him the heir of

Palladio and Schinkel; Schoenberg created a new musical language inspired by the Viennese tradition; and Egon Schiele, not easily accepted as a painter by his contemporaries, was searching for a form of artistic expression that eludes time. This great modernist wrote paradoxically in the corner of one of his drawings (1912): "Art cannot be modern, it always goes back to origins."

As Jean Clair has recently written, "between 1905 and 1918 Vienna was the center of a renewal compared to none, but this renewal, contrary to *Rinascimento* or *Aufklärung,* was not on the optimistic sign of Enlightenment: it [gave] birth to modernity and by being auto-reflexive it [acted] as a critical instrument of itself."[2] At the same time in Italy, the progressive avant-garde emerged with Futurism, again a movement that took the form of an "unequivocal critique of the *ancien régime.*"[3] But all through the first half of the century modernity seemed unable to reach its goal; it faced crisis after crisis and a major setback: the loss of acquired techniques.

Today the postmodernist critic is concerned with the rise and the fall of the modern avant-garde, with progress and mastery. *Modernism is dominant but dead,* according to Jürgen Habermas[4] who also maintains that modernism has not failed in its objective, but while it is still the official culture, it has become a tradition and has met with a historical limit. In this postmodern condition, the emergence of a world culture, more precisely of the coexistence of different cultures, has brought the uneasy feeling that our Western civilisation is confronted with a crisis of cultural authority and is nearing the end of a sort of cultural monopoly. The sudden interest in all forms of regionalism, where roots and origins are to be found, is not only a form of curiosity or a defensive measure but a tool to refine our sensitivity to differences. The result is that preserving a simple country farm in North America is just as meaningful for more and more people as contributing to the restoration of Venice.

The concept of our American heritage is related intimately to the search for identity, and it has gone far beyond the simple desire of preserving the past. While in the past it was associated with a certain folkloric view of obsolete values, the contemporary vision of the heritage is closer to reality, to a way of living that tends to resist the excess of urbanisation. It does so by trying to restore the old and the relatively old in the perspective of historical evolution and continuity.

The press has greatly contributed to the creation of pressure groups that are working toward an awakening of a social consciousness of preservation and restoration needs. These groups have succeeded in arousing an interest in the revitalization of old quarters, especially

**Old Towers at the Grand Seminary in Montreal, Canada.** *(Photo: Notman Photographic Archives, McCord Museum, McGill University, Montreal.)*

when their inhabitants can be convinced that they would enjoy better living conditions as a result. But the press has been less persuasive in lessening the indifference of the general public to major preservation issues such as the renewal of harbour installations, the remodelling of city centres or the intrusion of modern architecture in the old quarters of major cities.

In Canada very few daily papers offer, even once a week, a full page devoted to these problems. However, in Montreal *The Gazette* has sponsored regular weekly chronicles, especially those written by Andrew Collard, and *Le Devoir* also has a weekly article by Alain Duhamel, followed by general information on heritage preservation. Regular coverage by the press is in fact relatively new—it goes back to the beginning of the 1970s when the Quebec Commission for Cultural Properties was about to be established. Prior to 1970 sporadic interventions in favour of historic properties were undertaken by governments, while individual initiatives were primarily responsible for the conservation efforts deployed. David Stewart of Montreal, for example, not only restored the old military quarters on St. Helen's Island near Montreal but also the house of Jacques Cartier in St. Malo and numerous historical sites like the Château Dufresne and Stewart Hall. The systematic intervention of governments had been

**Porte Frédéric in the Louisbourg National Park, Nova Scotia.** *(Photo: Serge Jongué)*

strongly requested by heritage groups who had the support of journalists and writers at the end of World War II. The way forward was slow, but there were some major results; for instance the restoration of Louisbourg in Nova Scotia, undertaken by Parks Canada.

The primary purpose of the Quebec Commission for Cultural Properties is to preserve the best examples of the immovable heritage of the province. As an advisory board to the minister responsible, it gives advice on what cultural property should be classified, recognized, or registered, and how it should be preserved.

One of the most famous examples of mutual support between the press and the commission is a partnership that lasted nearly ten years, between 1972 and 1982. This was the case of Domaine Saint Sulpice, one of the landmarks on Sherbrooke Street in Montreal. It was first suggested to the minister in 1972 that it should become a historical district. In 1975 this recommendation had not yet been followed up and a second recommendation was sent to the minister. Again, political factors led to delays. The press became more and more inquisitive. In 1980 the announcement was made that a residential tower was to be built adjacent to the Domaine. Protection now became a matter of burning urgency; major articles appeared in *La Presse, The Gazette,* and *Le Devoir.* In May 1981 the minister finally signed an intent of classification within thirty days in conformity with Article 25 of the

Law on Cultural Properties. Using his privilege, the owner opposed this decision and expressed a preference to abide with a "plan d'ensemble" (master plan) for the City of Montreal. The commission gave a final recommendation to the minister in May 1982 and the Domaine Saint Sulpice was classified as a historical site.

The first question that comes to mind is why is it so difficult to obtain results when a cultural property recognized as being of major interest to a community is being considered for classification? On the part of the government, the question of cost is certainly a serious consideration. But when the government finally decides that the project is a priority and that funding will be provided, why does the owner oppose the intervention of the state by refusing the proposal? The answer lies in a lack of clear knowledge of the law and its privilege, and in the fear that to be classified as a historical district brings limits, freezes possibility of development, and is of the same nature as being expropriated.

The need for better information that could facilitate access to the origins of our civilisation and promote the establishment of cultural heritage policies has stimulated important studies in recent years, to mention only the Applebaum-Hébert report in Canada and the report by Max Querrien in France. Such studies point out how vital it is to include heritage protection as a principal objective in the development of cultural policies. Architects and urban planners still ignore it far too often in their work. Fortunately it is also true that in the last ten years the heritage concept has been more widely accepted by the public at large. We are asked less and less: Why restore this old building when it would be so much easier to build something new? The role of heritage magazines or of magazines publishing occasional articles on heritage concerns has been significant; they have focused attention on some of our most important historical properties and have also awakened the interest of young people. They have stimulated a passion for genealogy, for craftwork, and for design based on the transformation of traditional motifs. They have prompted many group efforts to revitalize a district, an old school, a church, an old fishery depot, a loft, or a natural site.

The battle for greater awareness of the cultural heritage must first be fought in the school, the ideal place to awaken young minds to the realities of history and culture. Most countries favour early contact with a pedagogy that teaches about civilisation, and no less than 10 percent of teaching time is reserved for that purpose. Assuming that school involvement becomes successful, and that the children are provided with adequate material (both printed and audiovisual) on their cultural heritage, it will be necessary to provide a better framework for the maintenance and sharing of such knowledge among adult populations. The traditional circuit of art galleries and smaller regional and thematic museums is not enough. The European "ecomuseum," America's natural and historical parks, and the heritage circuits of Ontario are among the types of institutions, based on an integrated policy of heritage interpretation, that offer a dynamic and coherent vision of history and cater to the contemporary need for knowledge of our shared heritage.

*Notes*

1. "The Mystic North" is the title of an exhibition held in 1984 at the Art Gallery of Ontario, Toronto.

2. J. Clair, *Considérations sur l'état des beaux-arts, critique de la modernité* (Paris: Editions Gallimard, 1983).

3. K. Frampton, "Towards a Critical Regionalism: Six Points for an Architecture of Resistance" in *The Anti-Aesthetic: Essays on Postmodern Culture*, ed. H. Foster (Washington, D.C.: Bay Press, 1983).

4. J. Habermas, "Modernity—An Incomplete Project" in *The Anti-Aesthetic*.

# The Canadian Experience in Heritage Preservation

JACQUES DALIBARD

There is a tendency among casual observers to assume that Canadians have learned to live with their long winters. People who hold that view have never been to Florida in February.

I too was in Florida last February. During my stay I made a pilgrimage to the Disney fantasy world known as Epcott Center. There is a Canadian pavilion at Epcott Center. The showpiece is an enormous movie screen that completely surrounds the visitor. As soon as he or she is properly in place, enormous Mounties thunder in from all sides. Energetic Eskimos practice survival skills. And spectacular mountains loom.

It is a presentation full of cultural symbolism. In my international travels on behalf of Heritage Canada, I have discovered that it is a vision still embraced to some degree by large numbers of people around the world.

This both eases and complicates the job of winning recognition for Canada's considerable heritage resources. It eases the job by evoking ready acceptance of positive statements concerning natural heritage, native peoples, and Mounties. But to some it brings blank stares of disbelief when we say, for instance, that despite our youth we actually take our heritage architecture seriously.

Until quite recently, it must be admitted, we Canadians have not been fully aware of our own heritage. Key events like the Montreal World's Fair in 1967—the event that crowned our Centennial Year celebrations—and later the 1976 Olympics drew not only the world's attention, but our own, to Canada's defining qualities and resources. A new consciousness is emerging. With it has come the determination both to protect the cultural resources that define us and to begin reaching out to the rest of the world.

I would like to review, briefly, the current status of cultural preservation in Canada, with special reference to the built environment. As Director General of the Heritage Canada Foundation, I would also like to share with you some observations on the role the foundation plays in preservation efforts. Finally I would like to share some observations on how Canadian experiences and innovations in this field might benefit other parts of the world.

### Preserving Canada's Built Environment

Every country faces some familiar—and some special—problems in preserving its past. In Canada, threats to the built environment, threats familiar to many of you, include a harsh climate and what might be called "development frenzy"—the wholesale destruction and replacement of older buildings in the name of economic revitalization.

In addition we have faced several preservation problems characteristic of young or recently developed countries: confusion in defining what our architectural heritage includes; limited public familiarity with heritage concerns; and a lack of legal and administrative structures to support serious preservation efforts.

The history of Canadian efforts to preserve heritage properties is very short indeed. Before World War II, the federal government's activities had been confined chiefly to the founding of several national historic parks—the first at Annapolis Royal, Nova Scotia, in 1917—and to the placing of plaques on key sites, many of which are connected with military events and buildings.

In the 1960s federal commitment broadened. The government expanded its efforts to acquire and administer sites that illustrate various aspects of the development of Canada. Today there are sixty-nine wonderfully varied historic parks across the country, ranging from the picturesque Fisgard Lighthouse on Vancouver Island to the fully restored sternwheel riverboat S.S. Klondike in Whitehorse, capital of the Yukon Territory.

Parks across the prairies include early outposts of the Hudson's Bay Company, the first European commercial presence on the northern part of the continent. In Ontario there is the two-hundred-kilometer-long Rideau Canal with its forty-seven lift locks, and early nineteenth century waystations and blockhouse fortifications. In Quebec one finds Les Forges du Saint-Mourice, Canada's first iron-making centre, dating from the 1730s. Artifacts unearthed during archaeological digs and reconstructions based on thorough scholarship recall that past. And Baddeck, Nova Scotia, boasts the Alexander Graham Bell historical park on the site of that great inventor's summer home and laboratory. These examples indicate the scope and variety of the historic parks programme. In addition there are nearly eight hundred historic sites, each identified by a plaque and an explanatory text.

Largely in conjunction with the parks and sites programme, the federal government has also greatly expanded its programme of heritage research since the early 1960s and has begun to fund the efforts of other agencies active in the field of cultural and historic preservation.

I should explain that, under Canada's federal system of government, the provinces and the central government have very distinct spheres of jurisdiction. The central—or federal—government has, for instance, the power to purchase and administer historic properties but does *not* have jurisdiction in the fields of culture, education, or the regulation of property. These matters, each of fundamental importance in heritage concerns, are provincial responsibilities. So although the federal government has been active since the 1960s within the limitations set by our Constitution, it has remained for the provinces to enact legislation applying *broadly* to heritage matters. With the exception of Quebec, this did not begin to happen until 1973.

Within its restricted mandate, the federal government assembled a world-class team of archaeologists, historians, architects, and engineers within Parks Canada, a branch of the Federal Department of the Environment, to pursue basic research. Their mandate has been to identify, record, document, and, where the federal government has acquired sites, to rehabilitate structures of historical importance.

In the process these experts pioneered or improved upon several important preservation technologies, including photogrammetry, cold climate metallurgy, wood preservation, underwater reclamation, laser cleaning of delicate surfaces, and computer-assisted recording techniques.

Let me mention just one of them—the computer inventory known as the Canadian Inventory of Historic Buildings. It contains detailed listings for almost two hundred thousand surviving historic buildings throughout Canada. It serves both as a source of current basic data on heritage structures and as a support for the designation and plaque-placing functions of the Historic Sites and Monuments Board.

The federal government, of course, also has responsibility for its own collection of historic buildings. Under the Policy on Federal Heritage Buildings adopted in 1982, it is committed to identifying, classifying, and preserving its heritage stock. As the federal government owns by far the largest number of heritage buildings in the country, this is a significant commitment.

Within the last thirteen years, each province and territory has also enacted some sort of heritage legislation. The type of legislation varies widely from province to province, as do the administrative instruments chosen, although most such legislation has grown out of "museum" statutes rather than "planning" statutes. Cities and municipalities are creatures of the provinces—they have no powers independent of the provinces. But in most instances the provinces have delegated powers to the municipalities to deal with heritage matters. The instruments now available to most major municipalities include:

- *zoning bylaws controlling the height, bulk, and use of buildings;*
- *plaquing bylaws;*
- *environmental assessment procedures;*
- *holding bylaws that give temporary protection against demolition;*
- *official planning acts;*
- *the power to designate heritage districts within which construction and demolition are controlled;*
- *design bylaws;*
- *limited powers to support renovation activities through grants, assessments, and tax collection measures; and*
- *public building revitalization plans.*

The private sector also takes an active interest in heritage matters. Commercial enterprise in the rehabilitation, cleaning, and retrofitting markets is booming these days, partly as a result of the recession and partly because of the greater value consumers currently place on these services. It is often more economical these days to recycle older buildings than to build entirely new ones. Some estimates place the value of rehabilitation work in the coming year in the five-billion-dollar range. This commercial activity is supported by a growing library of documentation, some very promising heritage trades-training programmes, and a steadily increasing pool of professional expertise.

In the noncommercial private sector, a bewildering variety of societies, agencies, and foundations has sprung up in recent years. At most recent count, there were approximately 850 officially rec-ognized groups of this sort, ranging from local historical societies to national museums and archives. Some are coordinated through provincial federations like the Federation of Alberta Heritage Societies or the Conseil des Monuments et Sites du Quebec. There are, in addition, seven major nongovernmental philanthropic foundations with an express interest in funding heritage-related activities. Partic-ularly prominent among these are the Devonian Group of Charitable Foundations and the Samuel and Saidye Bronfman Family Founda-tion.

## Heritage Canada

Two hundred and twenty of the most active of those heritage groups are member organizations of Heritage Canada. Indeed the founding of Heritage Canada in 1973 heralded, in many respects, the explosion of interest in the field. Let me briefly describe Heritage Canada's work and objectives.

There is a tendency among recently developed or developing countries to adopt cultural definitions articulated elsewhere. For much of the developing world, this has meant accepting European definitions. Much of Europe's architectural heritage consists of a magnificent assortment of castles, cathedrals, and ancient stone residences. It has therefore been the tendency of other people—and I include here Canadians—to measure the worth of their own architectural resources in these terms. By such a measure our past looks impoverished.

Heritage Canada began its work by embracing a quite different definition of "heritage." The previous definition had focused attention on a few buildings that could be restored as museum pieces. We, in contrast, say that restoring buildings as museums or museum villages is a worthwhile endeavour but a far too limited approach to conservation.

Our definition, therefore, is much broader. "Built heritage" is a fishing village in Nova Scotia with its brightly painted clapboard buildings seemingly located haphazardly but in fact well integrated in a landscape of earth, rocks, and water. It is a small town in Saskatchewan with its grain elevators next to the railway station, the very wide main street with its boom town front facades at right angles to the tracks. It is the warehouse districts of Vancouver, Winnipeg, Montreal, or Halifax, now hardly used as such but with a readily identifiable architecture and a unique character. It is a town within a town like Old Strathcona in Edmonton or Maisonneuve in Montreal with its institutional buildings, its main street, and its residential district almost intact and easily recognizable, giving a sense of scale, security, and identity to urban complexes that are often too chaotic and too big to make the average citizen comfortable. There are thousands of such cultural landscapes that properly constitute our "built heritage."

By this definition Canada—like other non-European nations—has a rich and valuable architectural patrimony. That understanding, in turn, becomes the springboard for a rational, all-encompassing programme of preservation activities. Within Heritage Canada, all of our

Hugging the rock-ribbed Newfoundland coast is a series of fishing villages known as Outports. The modest houses here are perfectly suited to their craggy and windswept environment. *(Photo: Government of Canada.)*

initiatives have been conceived within a framework set by that definition.

For instance an emphasis on vernacular architecture—on many buildings rather than a few—calls for broadly based public appreciation of such resources. For that reason we have directed our Communications and Public Relations Programme to the public-at-large. We have created TV advertisements that are shown on network media. Our magazines, *Canadian Heritage* and *Continuité*, are *popular* magazines rather than scholarly or coffee-table publications. We sponsor conferences open to the public and to the press. We are encouraging the celebration of a new national holiday, Heritage Day, on the third Monday of February each year. These initiatives flow directly and logically from the definition.

We value the industrial and commercial buildings that so often give shape to Canadian communities—banks, railway stations, manufacturing plants, and office buildings. We understand that key decisions affecting such buildings are made in corporate boardrooms and in the bureaucratic offices where tax measures, building codes, and property regulations take shape. For those reasons we have created a Government and Corporate Relations Programme in which we

Near the tiny Alberta town of Beaverlodge, an archetypal image of the vast Canadian prairie: gaily painted grain elevators stand in a row along a railway line. *(Photo: Government of Canada.)*

approach politicians and businessmen in every sphere to lobby for more sensitive decisions concerning heritage issues.

Further, we have embarked on joint ventures with private-sector firms to demonstrate the commercial feasibility of recycling older buildings and older districts. As befits our definition of heritage, we bypass museum pieces in favour of vernacular properties. We choose buildings that can be rehabilitated to make a substantial contribution to the preservation of the surrounding streetscape. We often make our choices with the intention of spurring other, more significant investment by the private and public sectors. We are thus able to achieve large effects through relatively modest investments.

We are acutely aware of the danger in this approach of getting ahead of ourselves—of creating expectations and demands that there is no expertise to fulfill. Architects, builders, and tradespeople who have skills appropriate to the enterprise must be available. This calls for professional familiarization and trades training. We have thus made it a priority to train the trainers, to ensure that a sufficient pool of talent is available to meet growing demands.

Perhaps most significant of all, the vernacular emphasis in our definition has lead to the Main Street Programme. We asked ourselves:

A one-time slum, Vancouver's Gastown is now a thriving shopping district thanks both to preservation law and to vigorous marketing strategies. *(Photo: Government of Canada.)*

where do you find the most significant vernacular architecture? In most communities you find it in the old town. You must, therefore, preserve the old town. Or, more to the point, you must ensure that its continued development is rational and evolutionary rather than quixotic, sudden, and massive.

The approach we have chosen is to participate in several demonstration projects across the country. Our objective has been to assist each community in revitalizing its commercial core through a combination of marketing and preservation techniques. We provide a fulltime professional coordinator. The town provides office accommodation. Merchants provide the investment capital.

The demonstration projects have been very successful. In each of the seven demonstration communities, the programme has generated new business, new jobs, increased prosperity for existing merchants, and an average of fourteen dollars of private investment for every dollar spent by the foundation. And, in keeping with our definition of heritage, revitalization has been achieved without sacrificing the integrity of the communities' vernacular architectural heritage.

The CN Tower and shiny highrises are symbols of the new Toronto. But Canada's most populous city is also textured by a rich stock of nineteenth-century structures, including the Flatiron Building in the foreground. *(Photo: Government of Canada.)*

The effects, of course, extend beyond the commercial core. If I may use a familiar metaphor, the old town is a hub. Radiating from it are the town's residential districts. These too become stronger as the hub is reinforced.

We currently have requests from more than a hundred additional communities for assistance in establishing Main Street-type projects. Eventually we will be able to share our perspective—and growing expertise—with the entire country. We feel that the approach may find applications in many other parts of the world.

Each of these several initiatives is intimately related to all the others. Nothing but a coordinated approach will do—each element supporting the others.

My only regret about this approach is that it began so late. We have already lost too many buildings. In some communities visual continuity had been sacrificed in the name of radical redevelopment. However, the major stock of vernacular heritage buildings remains. The prognosis for preservation activities—especially along the lines I have outlined—is very positive indeed.

## Ideas and Resources for the Whole World

Finally some observations about Canada's contributions, and potential for contributions, to international preservation efforts.

Through the federal government, Canada has consistently supported international bodies like the International Council on Monuments and Sites (ICOMOS) and the International Union for the Conservation of Nature (IUCN) with money, people, and technical services. In fact there was a time recently when professionals on loan from the federal government headed the secretariats of both ICOMOS and IUCN. Their special contribution, beyond that of providing good administration, has been to foster the growth of information exchange among member nations.

Canada is a signatory of the Unesco World Heritage Convention of 1972. There are currently seven World Heritage Sites in Canada—four of them natural sites, the remaining three cultural. The cultural sites include an important collection of Haida totem and mortuary poles on the Pacific West Coast, the largest and best preserved bison jump in North America, and the site of the oldest known European ("Viking") settlement in the New World.

In addition to federal government involvement, museums, universities, and private organizations like the Canadian Mediterranean Institute, based in Ottawa, have been active in projects overseas to uncover or salvage cultural remains. The range of activities—both in discipline and in geography—has been very wide indeed. There are Canadian archaeologists, museologists, and preservation technologists at work on almost every continent: at Mayan sites in Belize; at the Dakhleh Oasis in Egypt; at archaeological digs in northeastern Brazil; in the medieval port cities on the Yemeni coast; on the Tigris in Iraq were salvage work has begun in advance of the construction of a new dam; around the Mediterranean in Spain, southern Italy, Greece, and Turkey.

Canadians bring a very high degree of academic rigour and professionalism to these enterprises. They are increasingly in demand.

Private-sector activity abroad is more limited, but shows signs of steady growth. Canadian architects, planners, and renovation specialists are more and more frequently called upon to serve as consultants, both in the developed and developing worlds.

These are the major features that now characterize Canada's involvement in international heritage preservation. It is my belief, however, that Canada's special type of experience in preservation activities is a resource that the world—especially the Third World—will find increasingly valuable.

In certain respects it is fortunate that we have come so recently to appreciate our heritage and that many of our buildings are of relatively recent origin. It means that we started fresh, with the possibility of developing new perspectives and techniques. It means that we have more experience than most in preserving simple vernacular and nineteenth-century buildings.

Canada's sophisticated preservation technology certainly has applications elsewhere. For instance the technology of retrofitting older buildings to make them more energy efficient, without sacrificing their heritage character, is a Canadian speciality.

Because the scale on which we operate is more limited than in older and more populous countries, it has been economically feasible for us to lavish attention and exquisitely fine-tuned techniques on our relatively few heritage properties. A highly developed technology can be adapted or scaled down if necessary by others. Compromise technologies, on the other hand, are not so easily transferable. For this reason, among others, there is great potential for application of Canadian preservation technology abroad.

Earlier I mentioned other preservation specialties such as photogrammetry, computer inventories, cold climate metallurgy, and underwater reclamation techniques. I could extend this list to include novel planning, legislative, and regulatory approaches—experiments in *decentralized* administration. I believe that these too will find many applications elsewhere in the world, especially in those countries that begin with a relatively clean slate.

I spoke of Heritage Canada's Main Street Programme. The emphasis is on the preservation of vernacular architecture, largely through local efforts. This is an approach that can be used as easily in Tunisia or Peru or Sri Lanka as in Canada. What is more, I find that the intent and the approach embodied in that programme are readily understood in those countries. They are certainly more appropriate than the alternative approach of stressing castles and monuments. Here too Canada could play a useful role in sharing its experiences with countries at a similar stage in their pursuit of heritage objectives.

At the levels of both technology and philosophy, Canadians have a useful contribution to make. We have benefitted tremendously from the experience of others. We are now in a position to return the favour.

# Facing the Challenge
## The Monumental Heritage of Egypt

GAMAL MOKHTAR

Egypt has inherited a huge volume and a great diversity of monuments—Pharaonic, Graeco-Roman, Coptic, Byzantine, Islamic, or
modern—created from the fourth millenium B.C. to the nineteenth
century A.D. Because many of these have been neglected for centuries,
their preservation is a vast and complex challenge, requiring cleaning,
consolidation, restoration, reconstruction, and continuous general
maintenance, not to speak of the landscaping and layout of hundreds
of archaeological sites.

Today Egypt considers the preservation of these monuments and
sites to be a national priority. The task calls for vast resources in time,
manpower, and funds, together with the most advanced applications
of science and technology. The work has been entrusted to the
Egyptian Antiquities Organization, which has shouldered its responsibilities in the knowledge that the historical heritage of Egypt is a
part of the world heritage.

The work is generally done by qualified Egyptian specialists from
within the organization itself or from universities and other qualified
institutions. Egypt is a developing country that must devote its
resources to industrial, agricultural, educational, and other essential
needs. It cannot bear the burden of protecting this great monumental
heritage alone and therefore gladly accepts the help of governments,
universities, and other scientific and technical institutions from abroad.
Indeed we feel that Egypt, the cradle of human civilization five
thousand years ago, ought to be the home of every scholar, researcher,
and scientist today.

There are many dangers threatening the Egyptian monuments and
a host of factors that are liable to lead to their rapid deterioration.
Many important monuments, such as the tomb of Queen Nefertari
at Western Thebes, have been decaying for centuries. Others, like
the world famous Sphinx at Giza, are facing relatively recent deterioration.

Egypt's monuments are threatened by the expansion of agriculture and irrigation projects; by urban and housing developments, especially the encroachment of newly built up areas on ancient sites; by drainage from neighbouring buildings through capillary action; by industrial development and factory installation; by military establishments; by neighbouring airports and road traffic. Bold smugglers cut away and remove entire segments of tombs and temples. Tourism increases general pollution and vibration. Atmospheric pollution, insects and wild plants, sandstorms, rains and torrents, the desert climate and its great stress-inducing fluctuations in temperature, the high water table and its changing levels, the introduction of moisture into walls through the absorption of atmospheric humidity—these are additional factors of destruction. By far the greatest danger is salt crystallization due to the presence of water-soluble salts in stone, especially behind the surface of the stone, that peels away and obliterates reliefs and inscriptions.

Many measures have been taken to create permanent facilities to combat these dangers. Cairo University has established a department of restoration in its Faculty of Archaeology. The problem of uncontrolled urbanization has been tackled through a new Antiquities Law, which aims to limit construction on or next to archaeological sites in a strict but reasonable way. Measures to desalinate the rock structure, to control water movement into the stone, and to remove incrustations from the gypsum veneer have been developed. An archaeological survey of Egyptian monuments has been launched in order to establish priorities for dealing with damaged or threatened monuments, particularly those in long-neglected areas. Two documentation centres, one for ancient monuments and one for Islamic monuments, have been established in Cairo and have begun the task of complete scientific registration through photographs, facsimile drawings, photogrammetry, architectural drawings and descriptions, models, casts, etc. The Antiquities Organization has developed a Preservation and Research Centre to undertake analysis, treatment, repair, and restoration. Unesco has assisted this centre in the acquisition of new scientific apparatus. It is in close scientific touch with the numerous different schools of restoration and with the latest theories and experiences in the field. Pluridisciplinary cooperation brings together archaeologists, geologists, restoration architects, physical chemists, engineers, soil mechanics specialists, and others. A number of projects suggested by foreign associations and universities for the implementation of modern scientific and technological methods have been encouraged by the organization; for example, photogrammetric documentation, the use of cosmic rays to explore the second pyramid at Giza, the use of computers to order the forty thousand blocks of the temple of Aknaton at Luxor, and the treatment of the mummy of Ramses II in Paris.

Egypt has also sought to increase its limited economic resources through the promotion of tourism and tourism-related cultural facilities. Three major audiovisual programmes have been introduced at the Giza pyramids, the Cairo Citadel, and the Karnak temples. A fourth programme is being prepared for the island of Philae. All the entrance fees to sites, museums, and audiovisual spectacles, and all other funds related to the monuments are now deposited in a special account, which is used for the restoration and maintenance of the monuments.

It is against this background that I should like to mention briefly just a few of the preservation projects that have been successfully carried out in Egypt, whether by our own specialists working alone or in cooperation with overseas colleagues and resources.

Egypt and France together established at Luxor some seventeen years ago the Franco-Egyptian Centre for the restoration of the Karnak temples, the world's largest religious complex. Because the complex was erected over a period lasting more than two thousand years the centre has to deal with different styles, techniques, and various materials (limestone, sandstone, granite, alabaster, mud, brick). Nevertheless it has succeeded in dismantling and reconstructing many architectural elements. Salt crystallization is a very serious problem here, owing to the natural stone, the presence of a large quantity of water-soluble salts, the extremes of desert climate, and the vast fluctuation of the water table prior to the construction of the Aswan High Dam. The centre's scientific studies on this phenomenon will be very valuable when dealing with the temples and tombs of Thebes, which are in grave danger of disintegration for the same reasons.

In the same way, Egypt and Poland established the Polish-Egyptian Centre for the restoration of the temple of Hatshepsut at Deir El-Bahari in western Thebes (Luxor). This centre succeeded in consolidating and restoring the third terrace of the temple in more than fifteen yearly seasons.

The Cairo Citadel is a great walled city whose towers date back to the reign of Saladin (1169–1193). Its buildings and fortifications were constructed by various rulers from his time up to the time of Muhammad Ali (1805–1848). With its multitude of mosques, palaces, museums, and other monuments, the Citadel is considered the greatest monument in the Islamic world. An ambitious scheme was planned

**Cairo Citadel. General view showing mosque of Muhammad Ali, taken in 1913.** *(Photo: Courtesy Fogg Art Museum, Harvard University.)*

for its restoration and development as an eternal symbol of the most important periods of Islamic Egypt and as a cultural and tourist centre on a national as well as international scale.

A first stage of the scheme has been completed. The towers, gateways, walls, and aqueducts have been restored, together with the edifices of the Muhammad Ali period within the Citadel. Two towers and Joseph's well have been made accessible to visitors. The mosques of Muhammad Ali, Nasser Muhammad, and Soliman Pasha have been cleaned and restored. The El Gawhara Palace Museum, Guest Palace Museum, Royal Carriage Museum, and Antiquities Garden Museum have been established. Gardens exceeding forty-five thousand square metres have been landscaped. A restoration centre for Islamic antiquities and a documentation centre for Islamic and Coptic antiquities have also been set up.

Another major project concerns the Babilyon Castle and El-Mo'alaka church. The Coptic Museum building in Old Cairo and its archaeological elements, together with the archaeological area surrounding the museum—an ensemble representing Roman, Coptic, and Islamic

Cairo, Amr Ibn El Aass
mosque. Interior, looking
southwest to northeast, as
it was many decades ago.
*(Photo: G. Lekegian,
courtesy Fogg Art Museum,
Harvard University.)*

Egypt—were the object of a comprehensive plan initiated by the Egyptian Antiquities Organization. The museum required rapid specialized intervention. The restoration and development programme covered the Old Wing (1915), the New Wing (1947), the Roman Tower, the exterior gardens and facades, as well as the archaeological collections. The development scheme also included the establishment of new buildings to respond to the increasing needs of the museum and its visitors; these included a cafeteria, a ticket booth, and a gift shop.

The Roman Castle of Babilyon was built in 98 B.C. Part of the El-Mo'alaka church and the Old Wing of the Coptic Museum are built on top of the Roman Castle. The restoration work done here included structural consolidation by injection and strutting, together with the replacement of decayed stoned. The El-Mo'alaka Church, which dates back to the fourth century A.D., is also called the "Hung Church" because it was built on top of the Roman Castle. It is also famous for its unique method of construction based on palm trunks and palm leaf mats. Its structure has been severely damaged by subterranean water. In the same area other monuments under restoration include the Amr Ibn El Aass mosque (640 A.D.) and the Synagogue of Ben Ezra, which was probably first erected in the seventh century as a Mepite Church.

The story of Unesco's international campaign to save the monuments of Nubia has been told elsewhere. Termed "the greatest archaeological rescue campaign of all time," the campaign rescued Abu Simbel and Philae at a total cost of $72 million, of which half was borne by Egypt and half by international contributions. Apart from this financial participation, the area now covered by the waters of the Nile became the scene of the largest archaeological "dig" ever undertaken, with scholarly expeditions from over twenty-five countries. Different countries also undertook to cooperate with the Egyptian authorities in conserving other historical structures. Thus the Federal Republic of Germany took complete responsibility for saving the temple of Kalabsha, a project that involved the dismantling, removal, and reconstruction of more than thirteen thousand blocks, weighing from one to two tons. France and Egypt took responsibility for saving the temple of Amada, and Italy was responsible for saving the temple of Illysia.

Egypt for her part donated particular Nubian monuments—small temples—to some of the countries that contributed to the project. Thus the temple of Dendur was sent to the United States where it is displayed in the Metropolitan Museum of Art, the temple of Debud to Spain, the temple of Iafa to the Netherlands, and the temple of Illysia to Italy. Egypt also sent many exhibitions abroad to help promote the campaign. The exhibition on five thousand years of Egyptian history travelled all over Europe and also to Japan. The Tutankhamen exhibition met with phenomenal success in America, Japan, France, the United Kingdom, and the Soviet Union. Many other exhibitions of Pharaonic, Coptic, and Islamic art have travelled the world. All of them have played a vital financial role; they have created enormous enthusiasm for the Nubian Campaign all over the world and have greatly promoted cultural tourism to Egypt. This is entirely appropriate for an undertaking that saved the precious historical and archaeological legacy of Nubia and thus permitted coming generations to see, study, enjoy, and learn from these marvellous temples and objects that have come down to us from antiquity. It has been an ideal example of international understanding and solidarity for the preservation of our common cultural heritage.

# The Scourge of Illicit Traffic in Cultural Property

# A Threat to National Art Treasures
## *The Illicit Traffic in Stolen Art*

EKPO OKPO EYO

Art dealers and indeed museum directors have often argued against the very idea of restricting the movement of art works across territorial boundaries. Their argument is largely based on the notion that any product of a creative individual belongs generally to mankind. The truth of their argument, they point out, is borne out by the fact that the democratization of culture and the accessibility of cultural artifacts to all mankind are among the cardinal principles of Unesco. They emphasize the point that such processes make knowledge about the peoples and cultures of the world available to all, thereby helping to remove mutual suspicion among peoples and replacing it with mutual understanding and respect as the only true basis for worldwide harmony.

There is, of course, nothing wrong with this argument, as far as it goes. However, it becomes immediately questionable in its application to real situations. In real life the notion appears to be valid *only* as long as art treasures flow in from the "peripheries of the world" to the "centre" and not from the "centre" outwards. Benin bronzes should be seen in museum showcases in New York and London, but it is impossible to contemplate Leonardo's Mona Lisa or Velasquez' *Portrait of Juan de Pareja* in Lagos or Accra. No, the risk involved would be too great, the paintings would disintegrate in the hot climate, and, in any case, the people of the country would not have enough artistic sensitivity to appreciate such masterpieces.

If you think that I have chosen extreme examples to illustrate my point then ponder the case of an ivory mask in Benin, used there for three centuries, and then plundered in 1897. It had remained in captivity in London for only eighty years; but when in 1977 its return was requested for use as an emblem, a rallying symbol, of all the black peoples who had assembled in Lagos for the second world Black and African Festival of the Arts and Culture (FESTAC), the British Museum argued that it was too fragile to travel by air to Lagos and that the climate of Lagos was unsuitable.

## Cultural Deprivation and Economic Exploitation

Illicit traffic results in Third World countries' being systematically deprived of their cultural heritage and being economically exploited at the same time. Under many guises (for example, disseminating information about mankind by showing cultural artifacts from every nook and corner of the world in London or New York), we find objects of veneration being torn away from their spiritual homes to adorn museum showcases and private homes. When you see a Benin memorial head in a showcase in New York, it does not mean any more to you than its identification as a memorial head of a "tribal" king. But this same head was made as a documentation of a particular king and it occupies a particular position in the history of the Benin people. Its removal produces a vacuum in Benin history. It follows that with the removal of so many Benin memorial heads, the means of reconstructing or illustrating the history of the Benin kingdom has forever been destroyed. Museums of the western world—contrary to their belief that by hoarding artifacts from the "peripheries" of the world they are passing on information—are, in a very special and real sense, destroying the authentic sources of information they wish to disseminate.

In the past, missionaries, explorers, scientists, and colonial administrators were the principal suppliers of objects to museum collections in Europe and America. In many cases, the objects collected in this way were well documented; others were poorly or incorrectly documented. In the last several decades, this situation has changed for the worse. Whereas in the past there was some attempt to inform, now much collection activity is confined to economic exploitation through organized theft: the sole purpose is to make money out of the heritage of the poor nations of the world. I would like to illustrate this with a few recent examples from Nigeria. Those acquainted with the history of the looting of art objects from Africa will be familiar with the infamous British punitive expedition to Benin City in 1897. In this operation the Royal Palace was burnt down, precious bronzes looted, and the king banished to die in exile. Today not a single western museum that depicts African civilizations is without one or two Benin pieces. Yet the Benin Museum has to display third-rate pieces and casts and photographs of others that now adorn museums elsewhere.

Even the few Benin bronzes now on exhibition in Nigeria's museums had to be purchased abroad and brought back to the country.

As far as the present time is concerned, before 1981 there may have been isolated cases of thefts of museum objects from Nigeria, but by and large our museums were not the sorts of places where unscrupulous dealers found it easy to buy objects. Now the story is different, perhaps as a result of the awareness created by the success of the international exhibition Treasures of Ancient Nigeria. I feel I ought to tell the whole story here because of the many questions and issues it raises: first, the question of sharing the joy of art experience with the world—an experience museums of Europe and North America have always advocated; second, the nature of cooperation with art dealers; and third, the dilemma of a museum director in the developing world.

### The Jebba Female Figure

This bronze figure is the tallest in the medium yet recorded in Africa. In 1972, when I had just become Director of Antiquities in Nigeria, the Jebba figure was one of nine such works scattered in several villages along the banks of the River Niger. All of them were associated with Tsoede, the legendary founder of the Nupe Kingdom, and were tentatively dated to the sixteenth century. In these villages the bronzes were the foci of religious activities in which every villager took part. They therefore represented the collective identity of the people. The Jebba figure was kept in a small mud house, and by arrangement with the local chief the Department of Antiquities provided a caretaker to look after its safety. It was the normal practice for our staff to carry out physical inspection of these objects at least once a year. In that year, the other eight bronzes had already been inspected when a cable was sent to me from M. Cahen, director of the Tervuren Museum in Belgium, saying that the Jebba figure was being offered for sale. We immediately rushed to Jebba and discovered that a thief had indeed entered through the back room window and removed the figure. A trip to Brussels did not yield any information other than that the object was in Paris. No one was willing to say more. The figure has since been lost, and the people deprived of their object of worship. Because the theft was well publicized, the figure has yet to surface. In a frantic move, the museum itself was forced to remove the eight remaining figures and replace them with copies. Thus the people of Jebba have been deprived of their cult object, Nigeria has been robbed of one of her national art treasures, and the museums

Africa's tallest bronze
figure, stolen from Jebba
island, Nigeria. The
whereabouts of this figure
are as yet unknown.

of Europe and America have no information to provide to mankind!
Perhaps the Jebba figure has been tucked away in some dark corner
of a private home, or perhaps it has been melted down? Who then
gains by this act?

## The Nok Piece

The Nigerian exhibition Treasures of Ancient Nigeria: Legacy of
Two Thousand Years, first shown in Detroit in January, 1980, toured
eight American cities and also went to Calgary in Canada. This
exhibition was organized not only to dispel misconceptions about
African art but also to share with the world, in an appropriate manner,
the joy art lovers derive from viewing great works of art.

It happened that as soon as the show opened in Calgary a couple
of African runners together with a notorious New York dealer went
up to Calgary to sell an ancient terracotta figure belonging to a culture
that has been dated to between 900 B.C. and 200 A.D. Apart from the
fact that the exhibition was an instant success in Calgary, the director

of the Glenbow Museum in which the show took place, Mr. Duncan Cameron, was embarrassed to have the figure—which could only have been stolen—offered him for sale. Mr. Cameron had sat as an expert on various committees that worked on the preparation of the Convention on the Means of Prohibiting and Preventing the Illicit Import, Export, and Transfer of Ownership of Cultural Property (1970). Canada is a signatory to the convention, and Mr. Cameron thought this was the chance to test its applicability in his country. The Royal Mounted Canadian Police was alerted and the vendors subsequently arrested. Although the case is not yet settled, this happens to be the first test of the Unesco convention in the Law Court, and all of us are awaiting the outcome. This case has once again highlighted the magnitude of the problem of illicit traffic in art treasures and shows specifically how international cooperation may help in checking the flow. The Canadian authorities have already spent considerable energy and money on the case, and I gather they are determined to pursue the effort to its logical conclusion.[1]

### Pace Gallery

I visited the Pace Gallery in New York in 1980 and saw a Yoruba wooden figure with which I was familiar and which my predecessor, Kenneth Murray, had photographed in the field. I did not have the documented material with me, so I could not immediately present it to the gallery staff. When I got back to Lagos, I checked the archives. There was no mistake about it, so I decided to xerox the information and the photograph of the object and send them to New York as proof that the figure had been illegally removed from Nigeria. On receipt of the information, the Pace Gallery wrote back to confirm the piece they had was the same one we had documented; they claimed, however, that they bought it in good faith. How would they get their money back, they asked? My answer was that they should return the piece to whoever sold it to them and show him the documentary evidence we had provided.

Six months of silence elapsed before I heard again from Pace. What I heard was not about the Yoruba figure; instead I received a cable asking whether we had lost three Benin bronzes, a head connected with the cult of Oduduwa, a very fine fragment of sixteenth-century plaque, and an aegis. The Oduduwa head was pretty well known, but the museum numbers on all the pieces had been scratched out and their documentation destroyed. I called Pace from Lagos and asked for photographs, which they immediately sent to me. With the help

Sixteenth-century, seven-
figure bronze plaque
stolen from the National
Museum, Lagos, but
retrieved with the
assistance of the Pace
Gallery.

of these, I was able to trace the pieces in the set of museum catalogues
that are permanently kept in my office.

The Nigerian Security Organization was immediately alerted, and
they in turn informed Interpol. But Interpol was too slow, and the
vendor, a black American, demanded quick settlement with Pace,
failing which he would withdraw the items. I then decided to approach
the Federal Bureau of Investigation (FBI) in New York through the
Nigerian ambassador to the United States, and the pieces were
immediately taken into custody.

When arrested by the FBI, the vendor stated that the pieces had
been offered to him in his hotel in Lagos by two men. He did not
know what they were worth; packing and an export permit had been
arranged for him. Rather than prosecute, I thought it would be better
to use this man to get at the source of the theft, which looked like an
inside job. The vendor was given a free return ticket to Lagos and
free hotel facilities for one week in order to help identify, from among
the museum staff, the two men who sold the bronzes to him. He
refused to participate in an open identification parade but asked for
photographs of all the members of the museum's staff. These were
supplied immediately. Despite a one-week wait, nothing came of it.
The vendor cautioned us to proceed slowly otherwise we would scare
away the culprits.

We decided to exercise patience, but the vendor eventually refused to return the bronzes to Nigeria—contrary to our previous agreement that return would be a condition for nonprosecution. He had enlisted the services of a lawyer who demanded that his client's money, about $25,000, be refunded to him before he released the objects. These were worth $600,000 in the open market. We continued to exercise patience until he returned to Lagos, where he was immediately arrested by the Criminal Investigation Department. He then had no choice but to authorize the FBI to release the pieces to me.

In the meantime Pace again sent information that another bronze—a plaque illustrated in my book *Two Thousand Years of Nigerian Art* was about to leave Nigeria. After the first thefts we had taken a not very satisfactory inventory of our collection, but this bronze was physically counted in the storeroom. Six months later it was nowhere to be found, and a second inventory was ordered. It was during the second inventory that we discovered two manholes in the ceiling of the storeroom—so carefully camouflaged they were not easily detect-

Ododuwa bronze head stolen from the National Museum, Lagos, but retrieved through the intervention of the FBI, New York.

Sixteenth-century benin
bronze plaque stolen
from the National
Museum, Lagos, but
retrieved through the
intervention of the FBI,
New York.

able. When the police arrived, they traced the tracks to the locked
office of a staff member who had been accompanying the exhibition
Treasures of Ancient Nigeria. This man has since been arrested, and
the case is pending in court.

Pace, although knowing exactly where the bronze plaque had been
taken, refused to disclose the information. Instead they offered to get
it back for us if we could refund the money the buyer had paid for
it. The amount was $35,000, and the worth of the piece in the open
market was then between $400,000 and $500,000. This posed a new
problem: should we pay to recover what had been stolen from our
museum? I had planned to send photographs of the plaque around
the world. These had in fact been printed, but I was advised that if
I sent them, the plaque would either disappear forever or be melted
down.

### The Ife Terracotta Head

One factor in the decision of the Nigerian government to provide the
$35,000 for the retrieval of the bronze plaque was a similar incident
that occurred early in 1980. Sotheby's had advertised the auction of

a fine Ife terracotta head. I had written to inform them the head had been stolen from Nigeria, and that it would harm their reputation to be associated with the sale of known stolen property. The piece was withdrawn from sale and returned to the "owner." When the Nigerian exhibition opened in Detroit in January 1980, someone telephoned me at my hotel and asked if I would consider buying the piece for Nigeria since I had succeeded in stopping its sale. If I was interested, another person would call me to discuss the terms. I was confused, but ten minutes later a woman called and told me the piece had been taken out of Nigeria by a missionary thirty years earlier and that she had sent it to Sotheby's because she wanted a public museum to buy it. She was prepared, however, to let the Nigerian government have it for $150,000. I was enraged and pointed out how improper it would be for Nigeria to pay for a treasure stolen from its own territory. The woman then wanted to know what she could do with the piece. I told her she could do what she liked with it. . . . She thought I was the most callous museum director alive. The piece has not resurfaced since then.

### The Dilemma of Developing Countries

I began this paper by questioning the validity of the argument that museums in the "centre" of the world should be allowed to display objects—no matter how they obtain them—for the purpose of scientific and cultural education. The cases I have described above demonstrate how helpless and vulnerable the museums of the Third World are, to say nothing of their unprotected shrines and temples. No one would quarrel if museums in the "centre" asked questions about the provenance of objects that come to them. Is it not obvious that asking museums and cultural authorities in developing countries to take protective measures is simply not enough? For as long as there is a ready market in Europe and North America, stealing will not stop. Nigeria, for example, has a vast territorial boundary and the cost of policing it would be astronomical. Even if we were able to afford the security, the attraction of easy money can corrupt law enforcement agencies.

I have stressed the role of museums in this matter and have not mentioned the dealers. This is deliberate as I want to emphasize that if museums would buy properly, illegal art dealing would be reduced to a minimum. For no matter how rich a collector may be, all works eventually end up in public institutions. It is by refusing to buy what is illegal that we can hope to take the momentum out of a trade that is not only immoral but is slowly and steadily eroding the most authentic evidence of the being of the peoples of the Third World.

In conclusion I would like to quote Ava Plakins, who wrote about the National Museum of Nigeria in *Connoisseur* (January 1984): "It is especially distressing that this particular institution should suffer such woes, since it is one of the most professionally managed museums in Africa. Moreover, Nigeria itself had made serious efforts to enforce a strict ban on exports of major works of indigenous art. But there is clearly room for improvement. *It all makes one wonder how much artwork finds its way out of less cautious museums and countries and into the hands of less discriminating dealers.*"

Let me add that it all makes one wonder how much artwork finds its way out of the hands of less discriminating dealers into equally less discriminating museums.

*Notes*

1. See the following article by Ian C. Clark and Lewis E. Levy for an account of the court case and its disappointingly unsuccessful outcome.

# National Legislation to Encourage International Cooperation
## The Cultural Property Export and Import Act of Canada

IAN C. CLARK and LEWIS E. LEVY

On September 6, 1977, an act respecting the export from Canada of cultural property and the import into Canada of cultural property illegally exported from foreign states came into force. The purpose of this federal legislation is twofold: to ensure the preservation in Canada of the best examples of the nation's cultural, historic, and scientific heritage and to protect in Canada the legitimate interests of other states concerned with the preservation of their own heritage in movable cultural property. The Cultural Property Export and Import Act was drafted after research into some of the systems of cultural property export control then in force in various parts of the world, particularly in the United Kingdom and France. It was designed to utilize what we perceived to be the best features of those systems while avoiding what we thought might cause difficulties of implementation in Canada. It was also designed to permit Canada to become a party to agreements with foreign states or international conventions relating to the prevention of illicit traffic in cultural property.

### Export: General Principles

The method of control employed in the act was designed to ensure the cooperation of the collector-dealer fraternity in Canada. Experience in other countries had shown that without such cooperation no system of export control can work smoothly, efficiently, and fairly. The drafters of the legislation decided to follow, as very sound, the principles enunciated by Viscount Waverly in 1950 in his report for

Britain's Reviewing Committee on the Export of Works of Art, since known in the United Kingdom as the Waverly Rules:

*1. The state must retain the right to prevent the export of objects of high importance in suitable cases by establishing a delay period.*

*2. In every case in which export is prevented, the owner must be assured of an offer to purchase at a fair price.*

*3. Offers to purchase should be related to the market price wherever the conditions admit of a genuine and reasonable market price being arrived at.*

Briefly described, the Cultural Property Export and Import Act does the following things:

*1. It authorizes the government to establish an Export Control List of cultural objects of certain categories and certain minimum values, the export of which is illegal in the absence of an export permit or of a licence.*

*2. It provides for export permits to be issued by customs officers.*

*3. It provides for the appointment of expert examiners to view cultural objects for which an export permit has been applied, and to advise customs officers whether a permit should be issued or should be refused in the national interest as defined in the act.*

*4. It states that if a permit is refused, reasons must be given.*

*5. It provides for the establishment of a Canadian Cultural Property Export Review Board to review applications for export permits that have been refused on the advice of an expert examiner.*

*6. It stipulates that if the Review Board decides it is in the national interest that an object be retained in Canada, it may establish a delay period not exceeding six months, within which period Canadian institutions or public authorities may have the opportunity to acquire the object by a fair cash offer to the owner, but if no such offer is received, an export permit must be issued to him.*

*7. It authorizes the issue of general permits, commonly called bulk licences, for exportation to dealers and general licences for export that apply to all persons.*

*8. It establishes income tax incentives for individuals selling or donating cultural objects to Canadian institutions or public authorities.*

*9. It authorizes the making of grants and loans, when Parliament has made the necessary funds available, to institutions and public authorities in Canada to purchase objects for which an export permit has been requested or to repatriate Canadian cultural objects from other countries.*

*10. It provides procedures for the recovery and return to foreign states, that are parties to an agreement with Canada or are parties with Canada to an international agreement, of cultural property exported illegally from those states.*
*11. It provides severe penalties, including fine and imprisonment, for its violation.*

Prior to and during its consideration by Parliament, the substance of the legislation and the control system it proposed were the subject of consultations with representatives of the various interest groups; namely, custodial institutions, collectors, and the trade. While all those groups found some aspects of the legislation with which they were not in total accord, there was general agreement among them that the legislation was fair and had been designed to protect the legitimate interests of all concerned. Most people involved with movable cultural property in Canada would agree that a number of important heritage objects have left the country over the years, and that if Canadian public authorities and institutions had been in a position to purchase them, or even if they had been made aware early enough of the sellers' intentions to dispose of them abroad, those objects would have been kept in Canada. The Cultural Property Export and Import Act now ensures that henceforth an object of importance does not slip away unnoticed and that an opportunity is provided for considering whether it should be retained in Canada or not.

The concern of the designers of the act was to limit control to a minimum. After examining export control systems in force in other countries, we concluded that any inherent defects in them became greater as the number of objects potentially subject to control increased. Whatever arrangements were decided upon would have to be administratively practical because any attempt to be overmeticulous would defeat itself. We believe a workable system of export control must confine itself to limited, well-defined categories, and that such control has been least effective and most irksome when it deals with objects not of the first order of importance. The legislation envisaged, therefore, the control of objects that are in the national treasure category. The intention was to catch those things that should be controlled without creating a net so tight that too much would be caught, making the system oppressive or unworkable, or both.

The instrument selected to establish the basis upon which the system would operate is the Canadian Cultural Property Export Control List. It would set the ground rules. At its simplest, control would be applied to objects above certain age and value limits, but no attempt would be made to exert control over objects beneath these limits. The act would allow for changes in the Control List in response to the upward movement of prices on the market, or in cases where the control may have originally been set at too low or too high a level. Before examining the Control List in detail, the principles governing exclusions from it should be explained.

### Exclusions from Control

The act exempts from control objects that are less than fifty years old and made by a living person. Of course there are national treasures to be found in Canada that are less than fifty years old, but to try to safeguard them by the control system proposed was judged to be both impractical and undesirable. First, it would considerably increase the number of objects to be scrutinized. Second, any control of trade in objects of less than fifty years of age might discourage the vigorous, two-way traffic that brings recent, important works of foreign provenance into Canada in exchange for those that leave it.

Most Canadians would agree with the decision not to exert control over an object created by a living person. This would infringe upon that person's right to dispose of a work he has created as he sees fit. We believe that during an active, creative life an artist should be given complete freedom, and in fact be encouraged, to gain an international reputation. Furthermore, while an artist is living, his or her oeuvre is not finite and institutions that wish to select from it can do so in free competition with foreign private collectors, dealers, and institutions.

The control system may include objects not of Canadian origin. As in other countries that have adopted similar legislation, objects forming part of the cultural heritage are defined to include not only indigenous objects but objects of foreign provenance. However, foreign cultural property must have first acquired "citizenship" through time and association with Canada before its export may be even delayed. Even if an object is on the Control List, a permit must be issued forthwith by a permit officer, without reference to an expert examiner, if the object has been in Canada for less than thirty-five years.

Canadian collectors should not be discouraged from importing cultural objects from abroad in the future because of the thirty-five year rule. On the contrary, those who are astute stand to gain by doing so if they choose wisely and well, for, as will be explained later, an outstanding foreign object may be eligible for tax exemption as a result of a gift or sale to a Canadian public institution, whether export of the object is contemplated or not. In any case, for those importing cultural property, thirty-five years represents a lifetime of collecting during which time such collectors will have complete freedom to export. The applicant for an export permit, if he claims that the object has been imported into Canada within the last thirty-five years, attaches supporting evidence or makes a signed declaration to that effect. The permit officer will not question such information unless he suspects fraud and the permit will be issued forthwith by the permit officer in the same way as temporary export permits are issued.

If the proposed export is for some temporary purpose (for example, exhibition, loan, authentication, restoration, or research), the permit is issued forthwith by the permit officer. Temporary permits are also granted forthwith to Canadian residents temporarily residing abroad. If the permit application relates to a loan to an institution or public authority in Canada made by a nonresident, the permit will also be issued automatically by the permit officer.

### The Control System

Under the Canadian system, the export of cultural property is regulated by reference to the Canadian Cultural Property Export Control List, which establishes categories and age and value limits. The departure from Canada of an object falling within the Control List can be postponed if, as the result of an appeal by a person to whom an export permit has been refused by a permit officer on the advice of an expert examiner, the Canadian Cultural Property Export Review Board decides that it is a "national treasure" and that a reasonable delay period should be established. This enables interested public authorities and custodial institutions in Canada to purchase the object at a fair market price. If the object is not purchased within the time limits of the delay period, an export permit is granted. Of course if the applicant for an export permit has not bothered to appeal the refusal of the permit by the permit officer, the matter will simply end there.

The act sets out the conditions for the creation of the Control List, which may include "any objects or classes of objects" that it is deemed necessary to control "in order to preserve the national heritage." It sets out six categories[2] that provide the guidelines for the establishment of the list itself, and for five of the six the act sets minimum value limits, the exception being objects recovered from the soil, the territorial sea, or the inland or internal waters of Canada. Objects

Crucifix, anonymous,
nineteenth-century
polychromed wood
carving, Quebec.
Repatriated under the
Cultural Property Export
and Import Act and
donated to the Musée du
Québec. *(Photo: Courtesy of
the Musée du Québec.)*

below the minima cannot be included in the Control List. Therefore
no permit is required before exporting them. It is important to note
that these minima cannot be lowered without parliamentary amend-
ment, but when appropriate, higher value limits can be set, and these
can be changed by Order-in-Council as the market varies or other
circumstances dictate.

The Control List itself is a detailed and specific definition of the
classes of objects that are subject to export control, based on and
fitting within the very general categories outlined in the act. It is the
legal reference for determining whether or not an export permit is
required before cultural property may be exported from Canada. The
Control List also serves to define cultural property designated by
Canada for the purpose of any cultural property agreements with
foreign states relating to the prevention of illicit international traffic
in cultural property. The Control List divides cultural property into
seven groups that cover the following categories of objects: objects
recovered from the soil or waters of Canada; ethnographic art or

ethnography; militaria; decorative art; fine art; scientific or technological objects; and books, records, documents, photographic positives
and negatives, and sound recordings.

The control system is administered across Canada through fifteen
customs ports where customs officials have been designated as permit
officers. These permit officers act on the advice, as necessary, of some
343 locally designated expert examiners. Normally officials of custodial
institutions in reasonable proximity to the customs office or offices
selected in each province to issue export permits, such as the local
museums, art galleries, provincial archives, and university libraries,
are designated as expert examiners. Each customs office has a list of
these institutions. From the description of the object on the application
form, the customs officer is guided as to which institution he should
approach to obtain a professional opinion. Instructions issued regarding the duties and responsibilities of the expert examiners should
ensure that the act is applied equally across the country, while taking
regional or provincial considerations into account.

It should be emphasized that in drafting the legislation we were
concerned from the beginning about avoiding unnecessary delays. In
the case of an application for permanent export, if the permit officer,
who himself makes no artistic judgments under this legislation, sees
that an object is in fact subject to control by reference to the Control
List, he refers the application to a local expert examiner; otherwise,
he issues the permit. If the expert examiner believes, after applying
the criteria set forth in the act for judging the significance and national
importance of the object, that the permit should be granted, he so
advises the permit officer who will immediately issue an export permit.[3]
If the expert examiner advises that an export permit should not be
granted, the permit officer will not issue it and the applicant can
either keep his object, try to sell it in Canada, or appeal to the
Canadian Cultural Property Export Review Board.

The Review Board reviews the decision and applies the same criteria
to determine whether, in its view, the object really falls in the category
of outstanding significance and national importance required by the
act. If the Review Board decides that it does, and concludes that an
offer to purchase the object might be made by an institution or public
authority in Canada, it may establish a delay period of between two
to six months. If the Board decides that it is not likely that an
institution or public authority in Canada would be interested in
purchasing the object, or, in the event that it has established a delay
period and no fair cash offer to purchase the object has been made

within that time, it directs that an export permit be issued. There is a procedure for determining what is a fair cash offer to purchase in the event that the parties cannot agree.[4]

Provisions governing the issue of general permits and open general permits by the minister, as authorized by the act, are set out in the regulations.[5] The permits have specific purposes. A general permit, really a bulk licence, can be issued to a reputable dealer to alleviate undue hardship or interference with his business. Such a dealer, on application and in accordance with agreed terms and conditions, is permitted to export objects that, although they might technically be subject to control, are not in themselves of such importance that an export permit would not be issued if applied for. Of course this privilege can be withdrawn if it is abused. An open general permit is a type of permit applicable to all persons and is published in the *Canada Gazette* so that the interested public can easily be aware of it. These permits, in effect, create exceptions to the Control List while they are in force. For instance a particular class of object, subject to control, might be in abundant supply, and the ability to exempt such a particular class of object for a period, which might be limited, ensures the necessary flexibility in the control system.

The system of control is generally considered to be fair and equitable. Its success may be measured by the fact that there have been very few cases of persons who have tried to circumvent it. Its operation only affects objects considered to be of outstanding significance and national importance, and so it does not seriously interfere with normal trade or infringe unduly upon personal rights. It does not expropriate or confiscate property. If a person has applied for an export permit for an object considered to be of national importance, he either obtains a fair price for the object or at worst, from his point of view, export of the object is delayed for a period of a few months to provide time for Canadian custodial institutions and public authorities to ascertain whether the object can be purchased at a fair price and thus retained in Canada. There can be no doubt that the legislation demands close cooperation among all of the groups affected by it. Dealers as well as collectors must work closely with the private and public institutions that have the responsibility of preserving the Canadian heritage. It is felt this point cannot be overemphasized. Any system of export control has a public relations function, and it also has the responsibility of setting the rules of the game. The very existence of the legislation, with the incentives it contains, has encouraged the communities involved to work more closely together. At each stage of the control process, which as an end result only creates a delay period in order to allow a fair cash offer to be made, there are opportunities for the potential exporter and an interested institution to reach some kind of agreement.

## Funds Made Available for Purchases

Legislation that only creates delays and ties up capital will not gain wide acceptance. However, dealers and private collectors are not elements of the population that the act purports to single out as groups that must be controlled. On the contrary, the success of the system depends on their active cooperation. This cooperation would not come easily if they were constantly faced with a conflict between their own natural tendencies of wishing to see the best elements of the heritage preserved in Canada and their pocketbooks. Therefore the system provides funds to assist Canadian custodial institutions wishing to purchase cultural property at its fair market value when an export permit has been denied by the Review Board. The act gives the responsible government minister authority, out of monies appropriated each year by Parliament, to make grants and loans, as individual circumstances might require, to public authorities and institutions in Canada to help enable them to purchase such objects. Grants and loans may also be made for the repatriation of Canadian heritage objects that have already left the country and have since become available for purchase abroad.[6] In the period from September 1977 to April 1, 1983, 722 applications for export permits were processed, of which 172 permits were issued on the advice of an expert examiner; 5 permits were refused on the advice of an expert examiner, but the refusals were not appealed; 16 permits were subsequently issued by the Canadian Cultural Property Export Review Board on appeal; and 28 permits for permanent export were denied by the Review Board. Of the 28 objects of cultural property for which export permits were denied by the Review Board, 26 were purchased at the declared fair market value by Canadian institutions. In 24 cases out of the 26, purchase, on the advice of the Review Board, was facilitated by grants from funds made available under the act.[7]

## Canadian Cultural Property Export Review Board

The body responsible for regulating the export of cultural property, in accordance with the provisions of the act, is the Canadian Cultural Property Export Review Board, which is appointed by the government. In addition to the chairman, there are ten members, two of whom represent the public interest, with the balance representing, in equal proportions, public collecting institutions on the one hand and private collectors and dealers on the other.[8] The intention was to set up an independent body made up of individuals having a recognized knowledge about and interest in the Canadian heritage. The board is a body of professionals. Under the act it can call upon any expertise it wishes in making its decisions. It has access to people employed in custodial institutions and to those who may have recognized knowledge outside that community, and it can call upon any technical and special competence it may require to assist it in any matter in an advisory capacity.[9] The Review Board has three basic duties.[10]

The first duty of the Review Board is to review appeals from applicants who have been refused export permits for permanent export on the basis of the advice of expert examiners. The second duty of the Review Board is exercised when an owner and a Canadian institution cannot agree on a price for an object for which the Review Board has created a delay period. This situation only arises if the fair market value of the object established by the exporter is questioned by the interested institution. In such a case the Board, calling upon the advice of valuation experts, will determine the amount of a fair cash offer. If the institution in question accepts this evaluation and offers to purchase the object, but the applicant does not, an export permit will not be granted, and the owner must wait two years before applying again for an export permit. If the applicant accepts the evaluation but no institution is willing to purchase the object for the amount of the fair cash offer, then the Review Board must instruct the permit officer to issue an export permit. To the date of writing, the Review Board has not received a request from an institution to determine the amount of a fair cash offer during a delay period. The third duty of the Review Board arises out of the amendments to the Income Tax Act of Canada.

## The Incentive System

In addition to establishing a system of control of the export of cultural property, the act provides tax incentives to dispose of such property in Canada. The Income Tax Act was amended[11] in order to give Canadian institutions and public authorities a competitive advantage in negotiating for important works and to encourage the collector to do business with the custodial community in Canada. These amendments to the Income Tax Act exempt from capital gains tax certified cultural property disposed of to designated institutions or public authorities in Canada (i.e., those found to be technically and professionally equipped and responsible bodies). Since the act came into force, amendments have been enacted by the Canadian provinces in the area of inheritance taxes and succession duties so that provincial tax law in the matter of capital gains is now consistent with federal tax law. In addition, gifts and bequests for such property under the act are now deductible up to 100 percent of income. This places all designated institutions and public authorities in Canada on the same footing with regard to the tax incentives. It carries into effect the principle of the donor's right to choose the repository for his collection, wherever in Canada that repository is located and whatever its jurisdiction.

The tax exemptions are not restricted to cases where owners are attempting to export national treasures or to objects covered by the Control List. When cultural property is being disposed of by owners to their local institutions, whether by sale or gift, if the disposition is referred to the Review Board and results in the cultural property being certified (i.e., the Board determines the cultural property meets the conditions of outstanding significance and national importance under the act), the owners can benefit from the tax exemptions if the institution is designated at the time of the disposition. Thus national treasures less than fifty years old and made by a living person can qualify for the tax exemption.[12] In this way, the transfer to the appropriate custodial institutions of objects in the national treasure category of more recent origin, and of whatever provenance, is encouraged before they are subject to the export control provisions of the act. It also means that outstanding collections and objects, the individual components of which do not meet the minimum values of the Control List, are also eligible for tax relief on an aggregate basis. During the period from September 1977 to April 1, 1983, 151 Canadian collecting institutions were designated for general purposes under the act and 39 in relation to a specific cultural property. From the applications received by the Review Board during this same period, 1,823 Cultural Property Income Tax Certificates were issued, thereby facilitating the transfer of cultural property to designated institutions evaluated at some 82.5 million Canadian dollars.[13]

## Estimating Fair Market Value for Income Tax Purposes

It became evident from the first applications for certification received by the Review Board that there was wide variance among Canadian custodial institutions as to the acceptable means for estimating fair

Kwakiutl cannibal birdmask repatriated by the British Columbia Provincial Museum with a grant from the government of Canada under the Cultural Property Export and Import Act. *(Photo: Courtesy of British Columbia Provincial Museum.)*

market value for donations. Some institutions, contrary to accepted professional ethics, had established inhouse evaluation committees for this purpose, while others viewed evaluations obtained for insurance purposes as necessarily synonymous with current fair market value. Where dispositions by gift are concerned, the Review Board has taken the position as a matter of principle that, for all evaluations, applicants support their estimates of fair market value with appraisals obtained "at arm's length" from persons recognized as professionally competent and qualified for this purpose. In cases where the value of one object is in excess of $5,000, the Review Board has found it prudent to require two "at arm's length" appraisals. However, for fine and decorative art and for archival material, where agencies exist to provide an appraisal that represents the opinion of more than one professional evaluator, one appraisal that represents a combined opinion has been found to be acceptable to the Review Board. Another evaluation problem encountered by the Board that is worthy of note is the practice engaged in by some collectors of purchasing cultural property at the request of public institutions, with the specific intent of immediately donating it to those institutions. The Canadian tax authorities, like their counterparts in the United States, have ruled that if an object is purchased for donation and the gift is made soon after, its fair market value for tax purposes is equal to its purchase price and that any attempt to establish a higher value would be regarded as fraud.

## Repatriation of Cultural Property

In addition to the duties specifically assigned to it under the act, the Review Board makes recommendations regarding the purchase, from grants and loans made under the minister's authority, of cultural property situated outside Canada that is related to the national heritage. During the period from September 1977 to April 1, 1983, of the applications for grants received from designated institutions for the repatriation (or "patriation") of cultural property, 176 were determined by the Review Board to meet the conditions of outstanding significance and national importance. As a result grants totalling almost 6.3 million Canadian dollars were issued. It should be noted that the designated institutions involved participated financially to various degrees. The monies voted by Parliament have been used to supplement local resources and initiative.[14]

### Heritage Surplus Assets Agreement

A further duty assigned to the Review Board at the request of the minister is to make recommendations under this agreement[15] regarding heritage objects of national importance that are either less than fifty years old or are not included in the Control List but risk being exported from Canada after being declared surplus by an agency or department of the Canadian government. If the scrap or market value of the asset being disposed of is above the level established in the agreement and a collecting institution is interested in acquiring the property, the request is referred to the Review Board for a ruling on the asset's heritage significance. If the Board agrees that the asset meets the conditions of outstanding significance and national importance, it is transferred free of charge to the institution in Canada that requested the ruling.

### The Import of Foreign Cultural Property

There has been growing worldwide concern in recent years over the illicit traffic in cultural property. The act therefore contains provisions that make it illegal to import into Canada any cultural property illicitly exported from a country with which Canada has a treaty or which is party along with Canada to an international agreement concerned with the prevention of such illicit traffic. Action may be taken in the Canadian courts to recover such property and return it to the country of origin. However, innocent purchasers and holders of such property in Canada are protected, for it will not be taken and returned to the country of origin until the owners have been paid just compensation by the reciprocating state as determined by a Canadian court.[16] On June 28, 1978, Canada became the 37th member state of Unesco to accede to the 1970 Unesco Convention on the Means of Prohibiting

*View of Quebec across the St. Lawrence River*, oil on canvas by William F. Wilson, 1851. Repatriated by the McCord Museum with a grant from the secretary of state under the Cultural Property Export and Import Act. *(Photo: M. Newman/Photo Studios, London.)*

and Preventing the Illicit Import, Export and Transfer of Ownership of Cultural Property. It was the first state that is more of an importer of cultural property than an exporter to do so. The transfer of cultural property from one country to another is no longer a matter of indifference to the community of nations. By the Cultural Property Export and Import Act the Canadian government assumed its responsibility to act as guardian of the heritage of all Canadians, and by acceding to the 1970 Unesco Convention it has taken an important step in the recognition that this responsibility extends to the cultural heritage of all mankind.

No action has yet been requested to restore cultural property to Canada. In March 1981 the first request was received from a foreign government for the return of cultural property that had been illegally exported. The Mexican government requested the return of two pre-Columbian statuettes that had been illegally exported from Mexico and that were being held by Canadian customs in Montreal. The statuettes were subsequently forfeited pursuant to the Customs Act because they had been falsely described in customs documents. In the spirit of the recovery and return provisions of the Cultural

Property Export and Import Act, they were delivered to the Mexican Embassy in Ottawa for return to their country of origin.

In December 1981 the second request was received from a foreign government for return of a cultural object. The case concerned the importation into Canada from the United States, on December 1, 1921, at Calgary International Airport, of an object said to be an ancient Nok sculpture illegally exported from Nigeria. Two New York art and antiquities dealers and a Canadian associate hoped to sell the sculpture to a large Canadian company for US$650,000. The Canadian authorities were subsequently unable to find any person who purported to know when, and under what circumstances, the Nok sculpture was taken out of Nigeria.

The two dealers and their associate were arrested in Calgary on December 2, 1981, and charged with violating Subsection 31.(2) of the Cultural Property Export and Import Act. The Nok sculpture was seized. Subsection 31.(2) of the act provides that it is illegal to import into Canada any foreign cultural property that has been illegally exported from a reciprocating state. Nigeria has been a reciprocating state within the meaning of the act since June 28, 1978, when Canada acceded to the 1970 Unesco Convention on the Means of Prohibiting and Preventing the Illicit Import, Export, and Transfer of Ownership of Cultural Property.

The prosecution was conducted by officers of the Department of Justice. During the course of a lengthy preliminary hearing into the criminal charge against the three accused persons, eleven witnesses testified as to the facts surrounding the seizure of the Nok sculpture, the authenticity of the object, Nigerian export control laws, and the absence of an export permit from that state. The provincial judge who presided over the preliminary hearing held that Subsection 31.(2) of the Cultural Property Export and Import Act could not apply to any object exported from Nigeria prior to June 28, 1978. The judge added that the evidence indicated that the Nok sculpture was exported from Nigeria prior to that date. He therefore discharged the three accused persons.

The prosecution brought a motion in the Supreme Court of Alberta to overturn the decision of the provincial judge on the grounds that he had misinterpreted Subsection 31.(2) of the act, and that he had lost jurisdiction in any event due to the technical flaws in the procedure he followed during the preliminary hearing, notwithstanding the objections of the prosecution.

The motion was heard by the associate chief justice of the Trial Division, who agreed that the provincial judge had lost jurisdiction.

He said that under the circumstances he did not have to decide the meaning of Subsection 31.(2), but that in his opinion there was insufficient evidence of the export of the Nok sculpture from Nigeria to obtain a conviction. He ordered that the charges against the three accused persons be quashed. An appeal was taken to the Court of Appeals of Alberta, where it was argued that the proper decision the associate chief justice should have made would have been to remit the case back to the provincial court for a new preliminary hearing. This appeal was lost. The court made it clear that it did not think the prosecution had enough evidence to proceed with the matter.

The difficulties in proving the likely provenance of the artifact and its illegal export from Nigeria had been recognized very early by the justice officers. They had sought to overcome these difficulties by asking the government of Nigeria to provide further and better evidence to prove these facts. However, several requests, made not only through the Nigerian High Commission in Ottawa but also through the Canadian High Commission in Lagos, remained unanswered and unsatisfied. The reason for this was that no such further and better evidence was to be found. For this reason the Canadian authorities concluded that it would be fruitless to appeal the decision of the Alberta Court of Appeals to the Supreme Court of Canada. They also concluded that it would be of little use to lay new charges and start afresh because, owing to the fact that the case started three years earlier and had been taken up to the Alberta Court of Appeals, the prosecution would be faced with a constitutional argument under Sections 7 and 11 of the Canadian Charter of Rights and Freedoms, saying that this constituted an abuse of process and the authorities were attempting thereby to deny the legal rights of the three accused persons. This argument might, under the circumstances, prove to be extremely difficult to counter. This, coupled with the observations of the two higher courts on the evidence and the impossibility of obtaining specific evidence from Nigeria concerning the actual export of the Nok sculpture, caused the authorities to conclude that further criminal proceedings should not be begun. It was felt that further pursuit of the case would only serve to discredit both the 1970 Unesco convention and the Canadian legislation.

At the insistence of the government of Nigeria, the attorney general of Canada had also begun a civil action in the federal court of Canada for the recovery of the Nok sculpture from the two New York art dealers and its return to the government of Nigeria. To succeed in the civil action, proof of the illegal export of the sculpture from Nigeria would have to be produced. Because the criminal proceedings had failed for lack of evidence of illegal export and written notice to Nigerian authorities had failed to produce any better evidence, the attorney general decided that the civil proceedings should be discontinued. This was done March 11, 1985.

In June 1983 a third request was received from the government of Peru for the return of five pre-Columbian ceramics and a stone sculpture that had been seized by Canadian customs at the port of Toronto. The request was dealt with through the forfeiture provisions of the customs act, and the objects were returned to the Peruvian consulate on October 12, 1983.

A Greek icon was seized by the police in Victoria after having been smuggled into Canada in 1982. In December 1983 the Hellenic Ministry of Culture advised that the icon had not been legally exported. At the end of the fiscal year, however, the ministry had not asked that it be returned to Greece.

## Penalties

Under the act it is illegal, without a permit, to export or attempt to export from Canada any object included in the Control List. Second, it is illegal to transfer a permit to allow anyone other than the legal permit holder to use it. And third, anyone who wilfully gives false or misleading information in connection with a permit application or its use commits an offence. Importing into Canada any foreign cultural property that has been illegally exported from a reciprocating state or exporting or attempting to export from Canada foreign cultural property that has been imported into Canada and is alleged to have been illegally exported from a reciprocating state and in respect of which court action has been instituted by the Attorney General of Canada, is also illegal.[17] The maximum penalty is a fine of $25,000 and five years imprisonment.[18]

## Conclusion

The Cultural Property Export and Import Act, which has been described in very general terms, is a "package deal." It balances controls and restrictions with tax incentives. Insofar as export control is concerned, to be workable it had to be limited to objects in the national treasure category. For those involved in defining the scope of the control system, the choices were really not that difficult—to try to identify and protect the best of the Canadian heritage in movable cultural property. The communities at interest, made up of dealers, collectors, and curators are implicated to varying degrees. Experience to date has shown just how symbiotic the relationship between them is and just how important it is that these communities, which are represented on the Canadian Cultural Property Export Review Board, cooperate and work together towards a common interest in the preservation of the Canadian cultural heritage. This ultimately is in the public interest. They are doing so more and more, and in the process the Review Board has become a formidable new instrument on the Canadian heritage scene. The success of this approach to export control of cultural property may be measured not only by the fact that there is no evidence to date of any significant measure of attempts to avoid it, but also by the fact that it has been achieving its intended purpose with an insignificant increase in the public service. The legislation is administered by a very small office in Ottawa, and it has not been necessary for the enforcement of the act to increase the number of customs officers in the fifteen ports from which cultural objects may be exported from Canada.

## Notes

*The authors have updated sections of this conference paper to reflect the current impact of the Cultural Property Export and Import Act.*

1. The Cultural Property Export and Import Act, 23–24, Elizabeth II, Chapter 50.

2. Subsection 3(2) of the Cultural Property Export and Import Act: broadly speaking the six categories are archaeological finds, objects made by the aboriginal people of Canada, objects of decorative art more than 100 years old, archival material, fine art, and other objects that have a fair market value in Canada of not less than $3,000.

3. Subsection 8(3) of the Cultural Property Export and Import Act. The criteria are: (a) Whether the object is of outstanding significance by reason of (1) its close association with Canadian history or national life, (2) its aesthetic qualities, or (3) its value in the study of the arts or sciences; *and* (b) Whether the object is of such a degree of national importance that its loss to Canada would significantly diminish the national heritage.

4. Sections 23 and 24 of the Cultural Property Export and Import Act.

5. Sections 14 and 33 of the Cultural Property Export and Import Act.

6. Section 29 of the Cultural Property Export and Import Act. The act also provided for the creation of an endowment fund, the Canadian Heritage Preservation Endowment Account (Section 30), to accomplish the same ends as set out for the parliamentary appropriations. To date it has not been found advisable to implement this provision.

7. Figures obtained from the Canadian Cultural Property Export Review Board.

8. Section 15 of the Cultural Property Export and Import Act.

9. Section 19 of the Cultural Property Export and Import Act.

10. Section 17 of the Cultural Property Export and Import Act.

11. Sections 48 to 51 inclusive of the Cultural Property Export and Import Act.

12. Sections 26 and 27 of the Cultural Property Export and Import Act.

13. Figures obtained from the Canadian Cultural Property Export Review Board.

14. Figures obtained from the Canadian Cultural Property Export Review Board.

15. The Heritage Surplus Assets Agreement was entered into in 1980 between the National Museums of Canada (on behalf of the Canadian collecting community) and the Crown Assets Disposal Corporation, both agencies of the Canadian government. As a result of this agreement, objects such as the satellite Alouette II, various aircraft, and small vessels have been transferred to museums or other cultural agencies in Canada.

16. Section 31 of the Cultural Property Export and Import Act.

17. Sections 34 to 38 inclusive of the Cultural Property Export and Import Act.

18. Section 39 of the Cultural Property Export and Import Act.

# Closing Address

AMADOU-MAHTAR M'BOW

The organizers of this conference could not have found a setting for
the closing gathering that expresses more aptly than this magnificent
Air and Space Museum the immense challenge that the conservation
of the past poses to all societies.

For the past two days at the Hirshhorn Museum, participants from
a wide variety of backgrounds have discussed numerous aspects of
our common responsibility in this field. How is it possible to reconcile
the vital task of conserving the man-made environment with contemporary needs?—a more complex problem than architects and town-
planners often imagine and one that calls for economic, social, and
political choices that combine realism and imagination. How can the
latest technologies be integrated with traditional knowledge and know-
how, in order to make the best possible use of limited resources? How
can we promote a form of "cultural tourism" that will help those who
have created a heritage to protect it more effectively and enable others
to view it? How can the illicit traffic in cultural property be combated,
particularly in the "importing" countries, where enlightened public
opinion is calling for more effective measures to limit such depredations? If replies to these questions are beginning to emerge in all
continents, it is undoubtedly because advances in the United States
and Canada have made for a better understanding of the complexity
of conservation—a task that demands both global and decentralized
approaches, combining public and private initiatives and allowing
each community, each individual even, to assume a due share of
responsibility.

In approaching the problem of conservation, a question must be
asked at the outset; namely, what should be preserved and why? The
most ancient? The most recent? Those landmarks of our everyday
lives that, viewed from the standpoint of tomorrow's world, already
seem to belong to the past? As a result, no doubt, of the rapid changes
that characterize our time and of a greater rapport with the rest of
the world, we feel the need to leave our imprint upon time and
preserve for ourselves and our children the most representative works

of creative genius. Thus we find ourselves today in a museum devoted to a most recent past and to the most modern of adventures—an adventure that began with the Wright brothers some eighty years ago, in the age of our parents or grandparents, and is constantly being renewed as astronauts from a number of countries, now operating in space, carry out experiments whose significance we cannot yet grasp.

No one can deny that this past, at once so near and so topical, should be conserved. The cultural heritage—which the Constitution of Unesco and the numerous standard-setting instruments drawn up by our organization require us to preserve and enhance—is becoming ever more recent while the notion of the heritage is itself becoming increasingly broad. Whereas at the end of the eighteenth century the precursors of conservation—for the history of conservation is itself very young—built up collections dating back to Egyptian antiquity or the Greek and Roman periods, curators are nowadays responsible for a past at once more distant and more recent, reaching back where human life is concerned to the earliest prehistory. Conservation, it should be noted, embraces everything relating to the life and activities of man, having expanded to include the "architectural" and the "industrial" heritage, both of which are constantly being renewed.

However, conservation of the past cannot simply be an end in itself; it must also contribute to the task of shaping the future by providing children and adults—*all* children and *all* adults—with educational and training opportunities that foster their personal development as well as the advancement of their societies.

How fortunate young Americans are to be able to come here and study a past that is still so close to us and to find explanations for the miracles brought about by aviation and space technology. How many vocations must have been born within these walls. Unesco endeavours to awaken similar vocations by combining activities in the fields of education, science, culture, and communication so as to encourage, even in the most deprived countries, the creation of museums, however modest, that will contribute to the growth of knowledge and to the emergence of vocations commensurate with the needs of our time. These include art and history museums that renew the collective memory and help to strengthen cultural identity, and science and technology museums that shape the future through the horizons they open up in the field of knowledge. Education, science, culture, and communication are in this way linked in a vision that makes it possible simultaneously to grasp the past and embrace the future.

From the symbolic significance of the Air and Space Museum, let me turn now to certain problems in the field of conservation that the international community must endeavour to solve.

The first problem is that of monuments situated in areas of armed conflict. Those who, like myself, lived through World War II with its massive destruction of cultural property—I need mention only Cassino, Coventry, Warsaw, and Dresden—placed high hopes in the convention signed at The Hague in 1954 for the protection of cultural property in the event of armed conflict.

Thirty years after the adoption of the convention, certain of mankind's outstanding cultural sites are still in danger. The Hague convention, however remarkable it may be, does not enable Unesco, which is responsible for its implementation, to intervene—as the International Committee of the Red Cross can do—in situations where political complexities are involved. The magnificent exhibition on Angkor Vat organized by the National Geographic magazine at Unesco's headquarters illustrated, nevertheless, the need for urgent action to save from destruction a site that the Convention for the Protection of the World Cultural and Natural Heritage would certainly regard as "of outstanding universal value from the point of view of history, art, or science."

Another problem is that of the underwater heritage. Distinguished specialists, many of them from this country, have done much to forward scientific knowledge in this field and to develop the techniques required to identify, collect, and preserve this heritage, which can make an exceptionally valuable contribution to world history. The time has come, it seems to me, to step up these efforts by organizing systematic underwater excavations to recover and conserve the cultural treasures lying everywhere beneath the seas.

Essential also in my view are stronger measures to prevent the illicit traffic in cultural property. One of the most effective ways of achieving this would be the ratification, by all states, of the 1970 convention designed to strengthen the fight against such traffic. The fact that Canada and the United States have become parties to this convention is an important step forward. This has been a source of legitimate satisfaction to all those countries whose cultural property has frequently been subject to pillage. But too many "importing" or transit countries, particularly in Europe, are still not part of the system of international protection established by the 1970 convention. The ratification by them of this instrument would help to stamp out traffic that is particularly harmful to the countries involved since it affects their most precious asset, their historical memory.

I cannot close this conference without once again expressing

Unesco's deep gratitude to all its organizers. I should like in particular
to thank all the participants—speakers, journalists, and observers—
as well as those who have contributed to the conference's success—
the Smithsonian Institution, the United States Committee of ICOMOS,
and the National Trust for Historic Preservation.

On behalf of Unesco, I thank you all.

# Unesco's International Campaigns for the Safeguarding of Cultural Heritage as of November 1985

**Campaigns already completed**

*Dates*

| | |
|---|---|
| 8 March 1960 to 10 March 1980 | *Egypt:* International Campaign to Save the Monuments of Nubia. |
| 6 December 1972 to 23 February 1983 | *Indonesia:* International Campaign for the Safeguarding of Borobudur. |

**Campaigns in progress**

*Launch date*

| | |
|---|---|
| 2 December 1966 | *Italy:* International Campaign for the Safeguarding of Venice. |
| 19 May 1972 | *Tunisia:* International Campaign for the Safeguarding of the Archaeological Site of Carthage. |
| 11 January 1974 | *Pakistan:* International Campaign to Safeguard Moenjodaro. |
| 10 January 1977 | *Greece:* International Campaign for the Safeguarding of the Acropolis of Athens. |
| 28 May 1979 | *Yugoslavia:* International Campaign for Safeguarding the Cultural Heritage of Montenegro Devastated by an Earthquake. |
| 25 June 1979 | *Nepal:* International Campaign for the Safeguarding of the Kathmandu Valley. |
| 13 July 1979 | *Thailand:* International Campaign for the Safeguarding of Sukhothai. |
| 16 February 1980 | *Malta:* International Campaign for the Preservation and Presentation of Historic Buildings and Sites in Malta. |
| 20 March 1980 | *Haiti:* International Campaign for the Preservation of the Historic Monuments and Sites of Haiti. |
| 7 July 1980 | *Morocco:* International Campaign for the Safeguarding of the City of Fez. |

| | |
|---|---|
| 25 August 1980 | *Sri Lanka:* International Campaign for the Safeguarding of the Cultural Triangle of Sri Lanka. |
| 23 December 1980 | *Senegal:* International Campaign for the Safeguarding of the Architectural Heritage of the Island of Gorée. |
| 16 February 1981 | *Mauritania:* International Campaign to Safeguard the Ancient Cities of Mauritania (Oudane, Chinguitti, Tichitt and Oualata). |
| 25 November 1981 | *Viet Nam:* International Campaign for the Protection, Preservation, Restoration and Presentation of the Cultural Heritage of the City of Hue. |
| 3 March 1982 | *Egypt:* International Campaign for the Establishment of the Nubia Museum in Aswan and the National Museum of Egyptian Civilization in Cairo. |
| 13 May 1983 | *Turkey:* International Campaign to Safeguard the Historic Quarters and Monuments of Istanbul and the Site of Göreme. |
| 17 July 1983 | *Cuba:* International Campaign to Safeguard the Plaza Vieja of the City of Havana. |
| 19 December 1984 | *Arab Republic of Yemen:* International Campaign for the Safeguarding of the Historic City of Sana'a. |
| 21 December 1984 | *Democratic Republic of Yemen:* International Campaign for the Safeguarding of the Monuments and Sites of Historic, Cultural and Natural Value in Wadi Hadramaut and in particular the Architectural Heritage of the City of Shibam. |
| 13 June 1985 | *Bangladesh:* International Campaign to Safeguard the Ancient Monuments and Site of Paharpur Vihara and those of the Historic Mosque City of Bagerhat. |
| 27 August 1985 | *Guatemala:* International Campaign for the Restoration of the Architectural Heritage of Guatemala. |

**Campaigns in Preparation**

*Afghanistan:* International Campaign for the Preservation of Historical Monuments in Herat.

*Argentina, Brazil, Paraguay:* International Campaign for Safeguarding the Heritage of the Jesuit Missions of the Guaranis.

*Ethiopia:* International Campaign for the Preservation and Presentation of the Cultural Heritage of Ethiopia.

*Kenya:* International Campaign for the Preservation and Presentation of the Cultural Heritage of Kenya.

*Lebanon:* International Campaign for the Protection of the Archaeological Sites of Tyr and Its Surroundings.

*Uganda:* International Campaign for the Preservation and Presentation of the Cultural Heritage of Uganda.

*Peru:* International Campaign for the Safeguarding of the Architectural Complex of San Francisco de Lima.

*Tanzania:* International Campaign for the Preservation and Presentation of the Cultural Heritage of Tanzania.

# Properties on the World Heritage List as of 6 December 1985

| Contracting State Having Submitted the Nomination of the Property in Accordance with the Convention | Name of Property |
|---|---|
| Algeria | Al Qal'a of Beni Hammad<br>Tassili n'Ajjer<br>M'Zab Valley<br>Djemila<br>Tipasa<br>Timgad |
| Argentina | Los Glaciares<br>Iguazú National Park |
| Argentina and Brazil | Jesuit Missions of the Guaranis: San Ignacio Mini, Santa Ana, Nuestra Señora de Loreto and Santa María Mayor (Argentina), Ruins of São Miguel das Missões (Brazil) |
| Australia | Kakadu National Park<br>Great Barrier Reef<br>Willandra Lakes Region<br>Western Tasmania Wilderness National Parks<br>Lord Howe Island Group |
| Bangladesh | The Historic Mosque City of Bagerhat<br>Ruins of the Buddhist Vihara at Paharpur |
| Benin | Royal Palaces of Abomey |
| Brazil | Historic Town of Ouro Preto<br>Historic Centre of the Town of Olinda<br>Historic Centre of Salvador de Bahía<br>Sanctuary of Bom Jesus do Congonhas |

| Bulgaria | Boyana Church |
| | Madara Rider |
| | Thracian Tomb of Kazanlak |
| | Rock-hewn Churches of Ivanovo |
| | Ancient City of Nessebar |
| | Rila Monastery |
| | Srebarna Nature Reserve |
| | Pirin National Park |
| | Thracian Tomb of Sveshtari |
| Canada | L'Anse aux Meadows National Historic Park |
| | Nahanni National Park |
| | Dinosaur Provincial Park |
| | Anthony Island |
| | Head-Smashed-In Bison Jump Complex |
| | Wood Buffalo National Park |
| | Canadian Rocky Mountain Parks* |
| | Quebec (historic area) |
| Canada and United States of America | Kluane National Park/Wrangell-St. Elias National Monument |
| Colombia | Port, Fortresses and Group of Monuments, Cartagena |
| Costa Rica | Talamanca Range-La Amistad Reserves |
| Cuba | Old Havana and Its Fortifications |
| Cyprus | Paphos |
| | Painted Churches in the Troodos Region |
| Democratic Yemen | Old Walled City of Shibam |
| Ecuador | Galapagos Islands |
| | City of Quito |
| | Sangay National Park |
| Egypt | Memphis and Its Necropolis—the Pyramid Fields from Giza to Dahshur |
| | Ancient Thebes with Its Necropolis |
| | Nubian Monuments from Abu Simbel to Philae |
| | Islamic Cairo |
| | Abu Mena |
| Ethiopia | Simen National Park |
| | Rock-hewn Churches, Lalibela |
| | Fasil Ghebbi, Gondar Region |
| | Lower Valley of the Awash |

* The Burgess Shale Site, which was previously inscribed on the World Heritage List, is part of the Canadian Rocky Mountain Parks.

|  | Tiya |
|---|---|
|  | Aksum |
|  | Lower Valley of the Omo |
| France | Mont-Saint-Michel and Its Bay |
|  | Chartres Cathedral |
|  | Palace and Park of Versailles |
|  | Vézelay, Church and Hill |
|  | Decorated Grottoes of the Vézère Valley |
|  | Palace and Park of Fontainebleau |
|  | Chateau and Estate of Chambord |
|  | Amiens Cathedral |
|  | The Roman Theatre and Its Surroundings and the "Triumphal Arch" of Orange |
|  | Roman and Romanesque Monuments of Arles |
|  | Cistercian Abbey of Fontenay |
|  | Royal Saltworks of Arc-et-Senans |
|  | Place Stanislas, Place de la Carrière and Place d'Alliance in Nancy |
|  | Church of Saint Savin sur Gartempe |
|  | Cape Girolata, Cape Porto and Scandola Nature Reserve in Corsica |
|  | Pont du Gard (Roman aqueduct) |
| Germany (Federal Republic of) | Aachen Cathedral |
|  | Speyer Cathedral |
|  | Würzburg Residence with the Court Gardens and Residence Square |
|  | Pilgrimage Church of Wies |
|  | The Castles of Augustusburg and Falkenlust at Brühl |
|  | St. Mary's Cathedral and St. Michael's Church of Hildesheim |
| Ghana | Forts and Castles, Volta Greater Accra, Central and Western Regions |
|  | Ashante Traditional Buildings |
| Guatemala | Tikal National Park |
|  | Antigua Guatemala |
|  | Archaeological Park and Ruins of Quirigua |
| Guinea and Ivory Coast | Mount Nimba Strict Nature Reserve |
| Haiti | National History Park—Citadel, Sans Souci, Ramiers |
| Holy See | Vatican City |
| Honduras | Maya Site of Copan |
|  | Rio Platano Biosphere Reserve |

| India | Ajanta Caves |
| | Ellora Caves |
| | Agra Fort |
| | Taj Mahal |
| | The Sun Temple, Konarak |
| | Group of Monuments at Mahabalipuram |
| | Kaziranga National Park |
| | Manas Wildlife Sanctuary |
| | Keoladeo National Park |
| Iran | Tchogha Zanbil |
| | Persepolis |
| | Meidan-e Shah Esfahan |
| Iraq | Hatra |
| Italy | Rock Drawings in Valcamonica |
| | Historic Centre of Rome |
| | The Church and Dominican Convent of Santa Maria delle Grazie with *The Last Supper* by Leonardo da Vinci |
| | Historic Centre of Florence |
| Ivory Coast | Tai National Park |
| | Comoé National Park |
| Jordan | Old City of Jerusalem and Its Walls |
| | Petra |
| | Quseir Amra |
| Lebanon | Anjar |
| | Baalbek |
| | Byblos |
| | Tyr |
| Libyan Arab Jamahiriya | Archaeological Site of Leptis Magna |
| | Archaeological Site of Sabratha |
| | Archaeological Site of Cyrene |
| | Rock-art Sites of Tadrart Acacus |
| Malawi | Lake Malawi National Park |
| Malta | Hal Saflieni Hypogeum |
| | City of Valetta |
| | Ggantija Temples |
| Morocco | Medina of Fez |
| | Medina of Marrakesh |
| Nepal | Sagarmatha National Park |
| | Kathmandu Valley |
| | Royal Chitwan National Park |

| Norway | Urnes Stave Church |
|---|---|
| | Bryggen |
| | Roros |
| | Rock Drawings of Alta |
| Pakistan | Archaeological Ruins at Moenjodaro |
| | Taxila |
| | Buddhist Ruins of Takht-i-Bahi and Neighbouring City Remains at Shar-i-Bahlol |
| | Historical Monuments of Thatta |
| | Fort and Shalimar Gardens in Lahore |
| Panama | The Fortifications on the Caribbean Side of Portobelo-San Lorenzo |
| | Darien National Park |
| Peru | City of Cuzco |
| | Historic Sanctuary of Machu Picchu |
| | Chavín (archaeological site) |
| | Huascarán National Park |
| Poland | Cracow's Historic Centre |
| | Wieliczka Salt Mine |
| | Auschwitz Concentration Camp |
| | Bialowieza National Park |
| | Historic Centre of Warsaw |
| Portugal | Central Zone of the Town of Angra do Heroismo in the Azores |
| | Monastery of the Hieronymites and Tower of Belem in Lisbon |
| | Monastery of Batalha |
| | Convent of Christ in Tomar |
| Senegal | Island of Gorée |
| | Niokolo-Koba National Park |
| | Djoudj National Park |
| Seychelles | Aldabra Atoll |
| | Vallée de Mai Nature Reserve |
| Spain | The Mosque of Córdoba |
| | The Alhambra and the Generalife, Granada |
| | Burgos Cathedral |
| | Monastery and Site of the Escurial, Madrid |
| | Parque Guëll, Palacio Guëll and Casa Mila in Barcelona |
| | Altamira Cave |
| | Old Town of Segovia and Its Aqueduct |
| | Churches of the Kingdom of the Asturias |
| | Santiago de Compostela (old town) |
| | Old Town of Avila with Its Extra-muros Churches |

| | |
|---|---|
| Sri Lanka | Sacred City of Anuradhapura<br>Ancient City of Polonnaruva<br>Ancient City of Sigiriya |
| Switzerland | Convent of St. Gall<br>Benedictine Convent of St. John at Müstair<br>Old City of Berne |
| Syrian Arab<br>Republic | Ancient City of Damascus<br>Ancient City of Bosra<br>Site of Palmyra |
| Tunisia | Medina of Tunis<br>Site of Carthage<br>Amphitheatre of El Djem<br>Ichkeul National Park<br>Punic Town of Kerkuane |
| Turkey | Historic Areas of Istanbul<br>Göreme National Park and the Rock Sites of<br>Cappadocia<br>Great Mosque and Hospital of Divrigi |
| United Republic<br>of Tanzania | Ngorongoro Conservation Area<br>Ruins of Kilwa Kisiwani and Ruins of Songo Mnara<br>Serengeti National Park<br>Selous Game Reserve |
| United States of<br>America | Mesa Verde<br>Yellowstone<br>Grand Canyon National Park<br>Everglades National Park<br>Independence Hall<br>Redwood National Park<br>Mammoth Cave National Park<br>Olympic National Park<br>Cahokia Mounds State Historic Site<br>Great Smoky Mountains National Park<br>La Fortaleza and San Juan Historic Site in Puerto<br>Rico<br>The Statue of Liberty<br>Yosemite National Park |
| Yugoslavia | Old City of Dubrovnik<br>Stari Ras and Sopocani<br>Historical Complex of Split with the Palace of<br>Diocletian<br>Plitvice Lakes National Park<br>Ohrid Region with Its Cultural and Historical<br>Aspect and Its Natural Environment |

|  | Natural and Culturo-Historical Region of Kotor |
|---|---|
|  | Durmitor National Park |
| Zaire | Virunga National Park |
|  | Garamba National Park |
|  | Kahuzi-Biega National Park |
|  | Salonga National Park |
| Zimbabwe | Mana Pools National Park, Sapi and Chewore Safari Areas |

# Notes on Contributors

**Michael L. Ainslie** (*United States*) was born in 1943. He graduated in economics from Vanderbilt University and went on to study economic development in Europe, Africa, and Asia as a Corning Foundation World Travel Fellow. While living in Cincinnati from 1975 to 1980, he restored his Queen Anne house and a number of other nineteenth-century houses for commercial and residential uses. As president of the National Trust for Historic Preservation from 1980 to 1984, he encouraged the expansion of private funding for and the American public's involvement in preservation. Since 1984 he has been president and chief executive officer of Sotheby's Holdings, Inc., the parent company of Sotheby's worldwide auction and realty operation.

**Ian C. Clark** (*Canada*) is Canada's permanent delegate to Unesco and a member of Unesco's Executive Board. Formerly he was secretary general of the National Museums of Canada and, immediately prior to that, was the first chairman of the Canadian Cultural Property Export Review Board. During his current appointment to Unesco in Paris, he continues to serve as special advisor to the review board, a position he has held since relinquishing the chairmanship in 1978.

**Hiroshi Daifuku** (*United States*), an anthropologist by training, devoted a twenty-six year career to Unesco's cultural heritage programme. He was chief of the Sites and Monuments Division (later called the Operations and Training Section) in Unesco's Division of Cultural Heritage from 1967 to 1980. He is now a private architectural conservation consultant.

**Jacques Dalibard** (*Canada*) has been executive director of the Heritage Canada Foundation since 1978. Trained as an architect, he was Canada's first official restoration architect and in 1968 joined Parks Canada as Chief, Restoration Services Division). In 1968 he also founded the Association for Preservation Technology and in 1977–78 he headed the Historic Preservation Program at Columbia University.

**Cevat Erder** (*Turkey*), a classical archaeologist by training, has been director of the International Centre for the Study of the Preservation and the Restoration of Cultural Property in Rome (ICCROM) since 1981. He has been a professor in the Department of Restoration of Historic Monuments, Middle East University, Ankara, and was dean of the Faculty of Architecture from 1977 to 1979. He has carried out many consultant missions for Unesco, and his historical study of the development of awareness of the architectural heritage in Europe is soon to be published by the organization. He has also been a visiting professor at Princeton and Harvard universities.

**Roberto Etchepareborda** (*Argentina*), former editor of the *Inter-American Review of Bibliography,* died on April 9, 1985, in Falls Church, Virginia. An

Argentine historian, diplomat, and educator who until 1984 was director of the Department of Cultural Affairs of the Organization of American States, he had recently been appointed coordinator of the organization's programme for the celebration of the five-hundredth anniversary of the discovery of America, to be held in 1992. He was a member of the Argentine Academy of History as well as of several Latin American academies and professional societies. An authority on modern Argentine political and diplomatic history, his extensive writings included works concerning the history of the Argentine radical party, the military in politics, and Argentine international relations.

**Ekpo Okpo Eyo** (*Nigeria*), trained as an anthropologist and archaeologist, has been director of the Federal Department of Antiquities in Nigeria since 1968. He has participated in many international consultations organized by Unesco and other bodies with respect to illicit traffic in cultural property and the return of cultural property to its country of origin. He is the author of numerous articles on archaeology, ethnography, and art history and of *Two Thousand Years of Nigerian Art* (Lagos: Federal Department of Antiquities, 1977).

**Sir Bernard M. Feilden** (*United Kingdom*) was director of the International Centre for the Study of the Preservation and the Restoration of Cultural Property in Rome (ICCROM) from 1977 to 1981. He has been a practicing architect since 1949 and has numerous architectural restoration projects to his credit, including York Minster. His *Conservation of Historic Buildings* was published in the Butterworths series Technical Studies in the Arts, Archaeology and Architecture in 1982.

**Maximilian L. Ferro** (*United States*) is an architect and preservation architect. He is also assistant professor at both Boston University and the University of Vermont and has lectured at many institutions throughout the United States. Born in Italy, he earned his B. Arch. at McGill University, Montreal, Canada, in 1966. He has several publications to his credit and has been asked to write the first comprehensive U.S. college textbook on architectural preservation.

**Yudhishthir Raj Isar** (*India*) has been director of the Aga Khan Program for Islamic Architecture at Harvard University and the Massachusetts Institute of Technology since January 1986. He is currently on leave of absence from Unesco, where he is chief ad interim of the Studies and Publications Section, Division of Cultural Heritage and editor of the international quarterly *Museum*. He was trained in economics and social anthropology at Delhi University, the Sorbonne, and the Ecole des Hautes Etudes en Sciences Sociales (Paris).

**Lewis E. Levy** (*Canada*) is a member of the Bar of Ontario, Canada, and an officer of the Constitutional and International Law Section of the Department of Justice of Canada. He was a member of a small group of experts that Unesco brought together in 1983 to discuss and find solutions to problems caused by the implementation of the 1970 convention rules regarding the illicit import, export, and transfer of ownership of cultural property.

**Ronald Lewcock** (*Australia*) was appointed Aga Khan Professor of Architecture and Design for Islamic Cultures at the Massachusetts Institute of Technology in 1984. He has been a permanent fellow of Clare Hall, Cambridge University since 1976 and senior research associate in Islamic Art and Architecture at the Faculty of Oriental Studies of Cambridge University since 1972. The author of various books and articles, he has carried out many architectural conservation missions in the Middle East for Unesco.

**Albert Mangonès** (*Haiti*), an architect by training, has been the director of the Institut de Sauvegarde du Patrimoine National (ISPAN) in Port-au-Prince, Haiti, since 1970. He was the founder of Sites and Monuments Historiques in Haiti, the predecessor organization of ISPAN. He was the first recipient of the Stanley Goldwin medal awarded by the School of Architecture of Cornell University and has worked in Mexico and for the United Nations Secretariat in New York. The sculptor of the famous statue in Port-au-Prince, *Le Nègre Marron,* he is an honorary fellow of the American Institute of Architects.

**Amadou-Mahtar M'Bow** (*Senegal*) was elected Director-General of Unesco in 1974 and unanimously reelected in 1980. Born in Dakar in 1921, he is a graduate of the Faculty of Letters at the University of Paris. An educator, he was his country's Minister of Education from 1966 to 1968 and Minister of Youth and Culture from 1968 to 1970. A member of Unesco's executive board from 1966 to 1970, he was appointed Assistant Director-General for Education in November 1970.

**Gamal Mokhtar** (*Egypt*), archaeologist and Egyptologist, was director general of the Egyptian Antiquities Organization and Undersecretary of State for Antiquities. He is the author of numerous publications on the history of ancient Egypt and is a member of Unesco's International Scientific Committee for the Drafting of a General History of Africa (Ancient Civilizations of Africa).

**W. Brown Morton III** (*United States*) is a free-lance consultant in architectural conservation. He served in the Office of Archaeology and Historic Preservation in the U.S. Department of the Interior and was chief of the Technical Preservation Service Division. He was also a member of the Consultative Committee for the Safeguarding of Borobudur and has undertaken many consulting missions for Unesco and the International Centre for the Study of the Preservation and the Restoration of Cultural Property in Rome (ICCROM).

**Andrée G. Paradis** (*Canada*) is director and editor-in-chief of *Vie des Arts* and vice-president of the International Art Critics Association. She was a founding member of the Canada Council of the Canadian National Commission for Unesco. She was also chairman of the National Art Center Arts Committee and the National Capital Commission Arts Committee and a member of the Quebec Cultural Property Commission and the Canadian Cultural Property Export Board.

**Paul N. Perrot** (*United States*) is currently director of the Virginia Museum of Fine Arts in Richmond, Virginia. He was Assistant Secretary for Museum Programs at the Smithsonian Institution from 1972 to 1984 and director of the Museum of Glass in Corning, New York, from 1960 to 1972. He is a former vice-president of the International Council of Museums Foundation and was elected president of the International Centre for the Study of the Preservation and the Restoration of Cultural Property (ICCROM).

**S. Dillon Ripley** (*United States*) is Secretary Emeritus of the Smithsonian Institution where he served for twenty years as Secretary until 1984. Previously, he was professor of biology (ornithology) and director of the Peabody Museum at Yale University. Under his secretaryship, the Smithsonian greatly expanded its basic research capabilities through development of research facilities in astrophysics, and in systematic, environmental, and tropical biology as well as in modern, American, Asian, and African art.

**John Sanday** (*United Kingdom*) was both the architect and the project leader for Unesco's Hanuman Dhoka Restoration Project and subsequently coordinator of the programme for the Safeguarding of the Cultural Heritage of the Kathmandu Valley. He is now a free-lance consultant in building conservation and repair, based in Nepal.

**Ismail Serageldin** (*Egypt*) is Director, Western Africa Country Programs Department II at the World Bank. He holds a B.Sc. degree in architecture from Cairo University and M.A. and Ph.D. degrees in planning from Harvard University. He joined the bank in 1972, working in the Europe, Middle East, and North Africa (EMENA) Projects Department. From 1980 until taking up his present assignment in 1984, he was Chief, Urban Projects Division, for the EMENA region.

**Stephan Tschudi-Madsen** (*Norway*), an architectural historian, is Commissioner General for Cultural Property in Norway and Director General, Central Office of Historic Monuments. He is also chairman of the Advisory Committee of the International Committee on Monument and Sites (ICOMOS). He has been visiting professor and Regents Professor at the University of California and is the author of a number of articles and publications.